RUMI'S Songs OF THE Soul

CHANNELED THROUGH

Rae Chandran

ARTWORK BY

Yizhao Zhang

OTHER BOOKS BY RAE CHANDRAN

DNA OF THE SPIRIT VOLUME 1
DNA OF THE SPIRIT VOLUME 2
PARTNER WITH ANGELS
DANCE OF THE HANDS
ANGELS AND ASCENSION
WISDOM KEEPERS SPEAK

RUMI'S Songs OF THE Soul

CHANNELED THROUGH

Rae Chandran

ARTWORK BY

Yizhao Zhang

LIGHT Technology PUBLISHING

The information herein is for educational purposes only. The content of this book should not be used to give medical advice or to prescribe any form of treatment for physical, emotional, or medical problems without the advice of a physician. Should you use any recommendations in this article for yourself or others, the channel, compilers, and publisher assume no responsibility for your actions.

For more information about special discounts for bulk purchases, please contact Light Technology Publishing Special Sales at 1-800-450-0985 or publishing@LightTechnology.net.

Also available as an ebook from your favorite ebook distributor

ISBN-13: 978-1-62233-059-1
Published and printed in the United States of America by

Light Technology Publishing

PO Box 3540
Flagstaff, AZ 86003
1-800-450-0985 or 928-526-1345
www.LightTechnology.com

DEDICATED TO

All Celestial Souls

Acknowledgments

I wish to acknowledge several people who helped bring this book together without whose support it would not have been possible in such a short time. I wish to thank Nivedita Ram for editing and laying out the poems in a structured format. I also wish to thank very talented artist Yizhao Zhang who graciously agreed to sketch the art, bringing a breath of freshness to the book.

I also wish to thank our angel in Singapore, Sister Anne Choo, who graciously provided her thoughts and suggestions for each poem. In the summer of 2017, I became very ill and had to be hospitalized. This was just a day after Master Rumi started coming through me (August 21). Sister Anne sent daily healing energy and also organized prayer groups for me, which continued for several weeks. Because of this constant support, my healing was accelerated, and I continued to channel and bring forth the poems from Rumi. I shared these poems with Sister Anne, and she encouraged me with her insights and thoughts.

Contents

Preface

RAE CHANDRAN

In the summer of 2017, I experienced a feeling to connect deeply with the universal master Lord Melchizedek. I meditated on him for a few days, and one evening, I felt his presence beside me. He started downloading messages as thoughts of inspiration into me.

The first message was a prayer dedicated to All That Is. I started feeling his presence more and more, and I looked forward to this experience. On the third day, he announced that we would have a guest joining us, Master Rumi. I was overjoyed, as I have always enjoyed Rumi's works and I have visited his resting place in Konya, Turkey.

During the next few weeks (August 21 to September 15, 2017), Master Rumi appeared daily, and I felt his presence in my house as though he were staying with me. He brought forth more than sixty poems and asked me to share them.

What I noticed from all the poems coming through me was that they were like signposts leading back to us. They are messages to join with the Divine within ourselves. I asked him about this one day, and he answered, "It is time to come Home and join with the Family of God again, as it has been a long time — this separation."

During these sessions, I was also told that Lord Melchizedek is Master Rumi. I thank both these masters for touching my life deeply in a loving and gentle way.

Rumi on the Philosophy of Life

MASTER RUMI THROUGH RAE CHANDRAN

What is not known about me is that I was greatly influenced by the understandings and philosophy of the magi who were the followers of the sacred fire. I had thoughts put into my mind while I slept and during times of deep silence about the sacredness of all life and to accept all things in life without discarding any of it. I followed this and never gave up on finding God, for in rejecting any part of God, I was rejecting God entirely.

I had no thoughts on consuming meat and wine as the magi did. In embracing all things in life, I also embraced human frailties — love, betrayal, sorrow, and death. I came to see each experience as a part of the whole, and all experiences enrich and enliven our lives.

My writings reflect this, for my writings were not only for the noble people but also the hardworking people, those on the bottom rung of the ladder. Although I have been depicted in some writings as a man of means who used his influence to get things his way, this is not true. My interest was always to be as a bridge between people and God. This was my true intention of bringing forth my writings.

Now in modern times, people must carefully examine what supported them before and make adjustments and corrections wherever necessary. I wanted to bring my writings in a newer form that would suit your present Earth reality because of the changing times and planetary shift. To do this, I chose my old student, Rae (he was one of the students at the seminary in Konya), to bring forth this new understanding to helping people remember the Law of One and the Family of God.

I offer these poems in humble gratitude.

Poetry

THROUGH

RAE CHANDRAN

MASTER RUMI ON

The Celestial Home

Like a sword in the hands of a brave warrior, I stand with my blazing torch and touch the intense darkness of my being.
I begin to see initially, partially, and then more clearly that I created all the darkness, for I was afraid, and in my fear, I kept creating darkness for me and others.
I felt false comfort in the darkness without knowing that it enveloped me and held me prisoner.

Now I stand in the blazing truth of my soul — the truth my soul has always offered but I did not see, for I was addicted to darkness and emptiness.
Now I claim it, and this bright torch of my soul shines like a brilliant sun on all the darkness I have kept hidden, a secret
As the light pierces this intense darkness, I realize that it was all self-creation; there was never any darkness, only a lack of love.

Now I am no longer afraid to look within, and I no longer seek or want anything. I know that all I want is within me.
Through this knowing, I can create whatever I need.

My light also showed me my shadow and how I was hiding from this part of myself that I had not accepted.
My soul gently whispers to embrace this unloved part of me. As I do, the remaining darkness disappears.
Now I am ready to embrace and wear the full gear of my beloved soul, for my beloved soul is the lover I have sought for eternity.
I adorn the finest dress of my being and step into the grand palace of my heart chamber. My beloved waits for me with all the splendor of a regal bride.
As our eyes lock in the eternal moment of now, I lose myself in the arms of my beloved soul, who has carried me to the threshold of heaven where the stars dance — the place the angels and masters call Home — for now I have become one of them.
I am Home now. I am Home now. I am Home now.

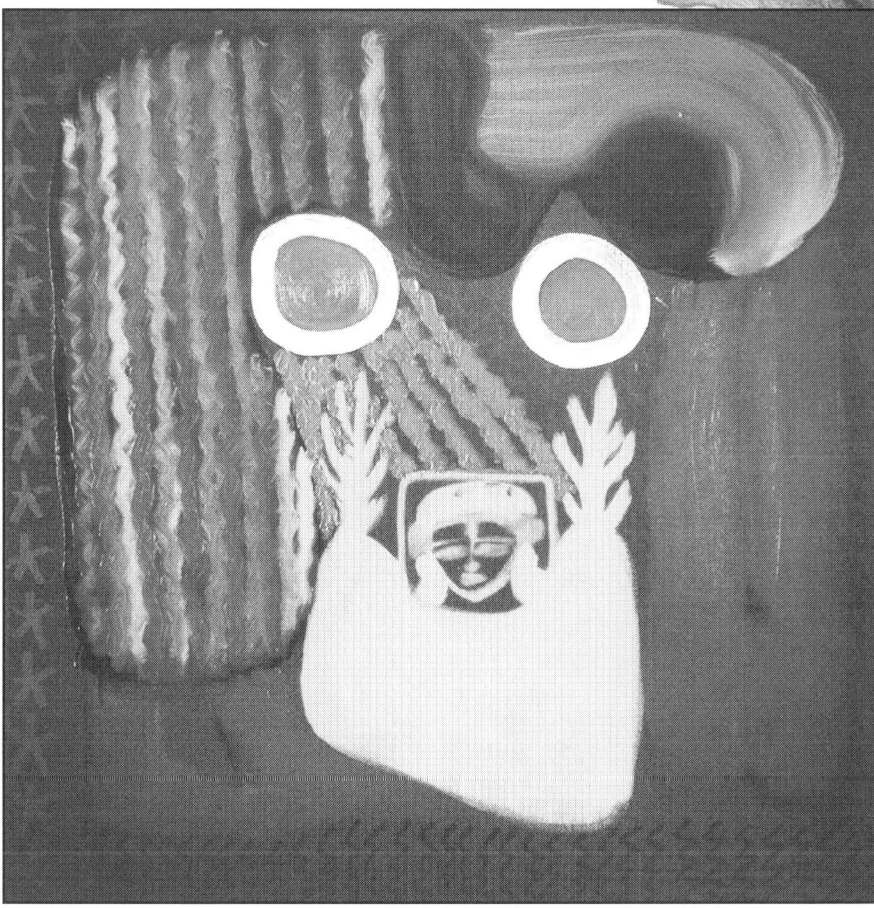

My home is love.
My home is truth.
My home is faith and trust.
My home is wisdom and peace.
My home is joy and the celebration of All That Is
My home is who I am.

MASTER RUMI ON

Challenges and Difficulties

Before a big rain, there is thunder and lightning, and it is scary to see the sky become dark and cloudy. Then the heavens let loose, and the waters fall.
After the deluge, all is clear, and a beautiful rainbow appears. The birds sing once again, lovers hold hands as they walk, saying how beautiful the rainbow is and that the flowers look refreshed.
The grass feels wet under your feet, but you walk on, saying everything is beautiful, refreshed, and recharged.
I notice how lovely it is, and this brings much lightness and joy into my heart. I sing a song of joy, for I know now that without the thunder and heavy downpour, rainbows cannot appear.
I make a promise to myself that from now on I will welcome all the thunder and darkness falling on my head, because I know at the end, there is always a beautiful rainbow.

So I begin calling thunder and lightning my friends, and slowly I notice that the thunder and lightning become less frequent, and the rainbows increase in size and frequency.
Then I dance in joy and ecstasy, knowing that rainbows and I have become one.

So, my dear souls, welcome all that life has to offer — the joy and the pain — for it is through these that your soul grows. Your soul wishes to know all its infinite expressions through its countless deaths and rebirths.

Pain is a process of growth whereas suffering is a negative thought embedded in the mind. Pain and suffering are two distinct things, and when you eliminate false thinking, you will eliminate suffering.

Life is a process of self-discovery, and through this discovery, you will realize who you truly are — a divine soul clothed in a human garment.

Blessed be. Though a soul, you cannot know your magnificence without the human body. So honor the body; it is a vehicle through which you gain freedom for the soul to reach eternity.

MASTER RUMI ON

Colors

Colors are the rhythm and the heartbeat of the universe. Where there is no color, life cannot exist in its present form.
Colors feed your soul and heart. Colors soothe your heart, lungs, kidney, intestines — all of your body — for the colors feed your I Am presence.

Partake the food of colors daily to see your life grow, and you will create harmony and peace in your life.
In each color, there is a secret the soul wants to decode and bring forth, for there are stories, music, geometry, and well-being in colors.

Each color you see — for example, red, blue, or white — are not just single colors but also reflections of a larger reality. Once you know this secret, you will understand the secret of the universe.

You are birthed and protected by colors within the womb of your mother. You experience soft yellow when you were in your mother's womb, which protects you and nourishes you.
There are colors for each of your organs and your entire body. Learn this secret from your soul, and you will never need to see a doctor again, for you will know how to bring balance using colors.

The universe is filled with color — from the grandeur of natural landscapes to the starry skies — and teeming with beauty and vibrancy.
Because you are part of this grand universe, you are filled with colors and vibrancy much more than you can see and experience.
I will tell you a secret: There are more than 144 colors in your palette, and all sing a glorified and unified harmony.

Be still and listen to this symphony, and you will begin to see the colors in all their glory and in all their hues. You will weep with joy as you see the incredible magnificence of who you are.

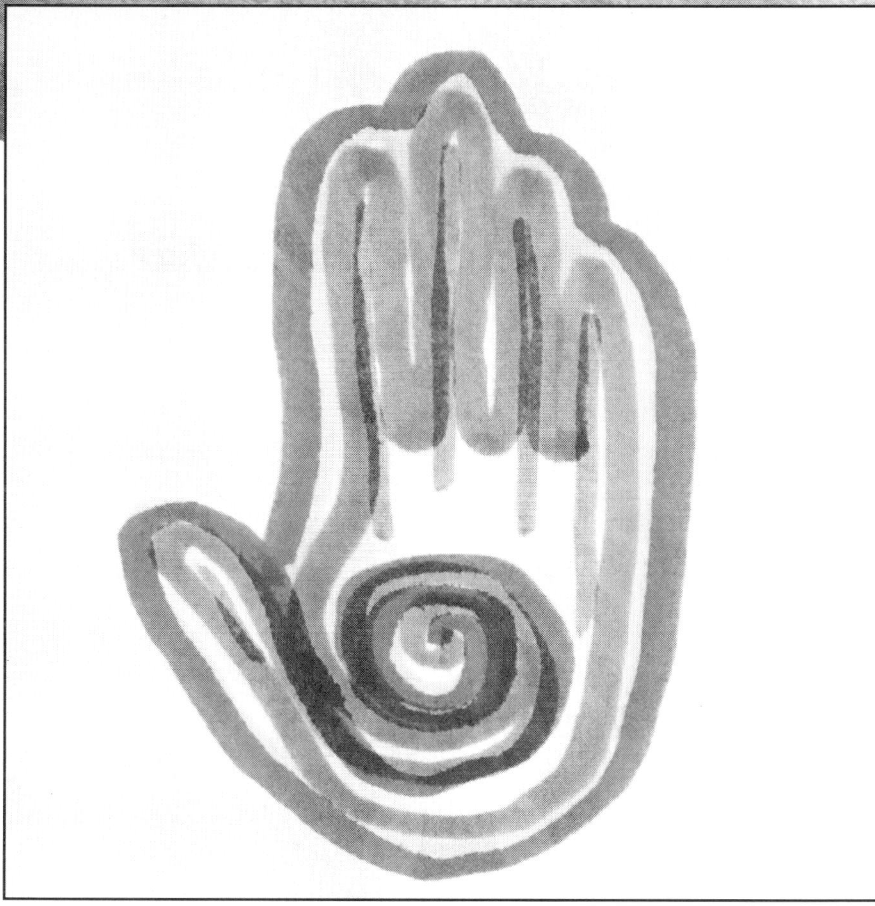

In this, you will begin to slowly start accepting yourself and the God within you, because you are indeed God expressing yourself in myriad details and through all colors.

MASTER RUMI ON

Dance

Dance is the expression of God in physical form.
Dance originated from the heart and mind of God. It was a gift to humanity for self-expression and to awaken the creative power embedded in the energy centers you call chakras.

By moving your body, you express your inner divinity or any other expression of life you choose to exhibit. In so doing, you create a story — a tapestry of life — in which many characters can be expressed simultaneously.

Dance is the breath of life, the breath of God.
Lovers dance to express their love for each other, and children dance to express their joy and happiness.
Your four-legged brothers and sisters dance to express love and solidarity, and the flowers and plants dance to celebrate their existence and beauty. And nature dances to expresses its magnificence through its varying colors, sounds, and seasons.

Waves dance on the ocean to display fluidity and oneness, and the dolphins and whales dance in the making and honoring of their community.
Birds dance in the expression of flight and freedom, and God dances in the celebration of humanity and creation.
So I invite you to the dance floor to move your body; dance and chase away your inner demons and worries to rediscover your inner divinity.

So dance to the many rhythms of life, in good times and challenging times, for dancing can be a healing balm for many.

Dance to the sound of music.
Dance in silence.
Dance in union or by yourself, but dance nonetheless.
In this, the burden of life may look solvable and manageable.

MASTER RUMI ON

Divine Lovers

Like anxious lovers wait for their beloveds, I too waited with bated breath for my divine lover to appear. And when my divine lover appeared, I could not behold such magnificence, for my divine lover's brightness was like a shining sun that I could hardly gaze upon.

My beloved whispered, "Come closer to me so that I can whisper in your ear and sing to you a beautiful lullaby, for I have waited for an eternity for this moment. And now it is here.

"Arise and embrace your magnificence, for we will never part again, you and I. This reunion and remembrance is part of our sacred contract — the promise we have made to each other, that which has been scripted long past.

"Now in this union, let us dance to life and its melodies, which will catapult us toward the mysteries of life and death.

"We could dance upon the stars and the universe, and we will become the stars and twinkle brightly. Our twinkling will awaken many.

"Our journey together has just begun, for there is magic to explore and mysteries to solve, for our journey will be not just for us but also for our brothers and sisters.

"Our journey will contain many steep mountains, deep valleys, and green pastures, and we will conquer it all with our strength and hope.

"Our journey will be a model for others — for our brothers and sisters — to follow. They will see our struggles and triumphs, and it will give them hope and strength to follow their paths, and the world will become a better place of love, sharing, and compassion."

In this modeling, I will fulfill my dharma.

MASTER RUMI ON

God

God, the omnipresence — the "omnipotent," a word used callously by all to describe the indescribable and claim it to be true and infallible.

By arguing and killing in the name of God and people claiming their God as the just and loving God and others' God to be blasphemous and silly, God has been made into a buffoon and given human character. We have made God in the image of humanity and given God human attributes.

"Alas, how did this come about?" I wondered aloud, and with a sigh, I gave up. My loving God was made into something of which I have no control.

So I surrendered into stillness, and I asked my God about this.

The answer was simple: "I did not create any of this. It all came from the fertile imaginations of the human mind."

Then I ventured to ask, "Is there any truth to all this?"

Again, the answer was very simple: "As a man thinks and believes, he will create so."

I asked, "Is there any way humanity will come out of this ignorance and darkness? I see great wars and killings happening in the name of God."

Again, the answer was very simple: "Choose to be and experience the God within you."

Then I asked, "What is this God?"

The answer was simple: "Love."

I yearned to be this love, this God, and I asked, "How can I be that which you are?"

The answer was again simple: "You and I are the same."

I understood this, and I said, "I will be that I will be."

The answer was, "So shall you experience that which you claim to be true."

In this understanding, my heart exploded in a cacophony of color and joyful celebration, for I knew that I am God/Goddess, indeed.

I keep this knowing to myself, and when I see others, I know in my heart that they are God/Goddess too. In this, I honor, respect, and love them, and most important of all, I accept them as they are.

MASTER RUMI ON

Happiness

Happiness — what is it?

It is what everyone wants, fights for, and looks for everywhere. Is it euphoria or something else?

Happiness is who you are, and it is a frame of mind. Who you are is determined by the choices you make on a moment-by-moment basis. The choices you make determine the quality of happiness you experience.

Happiness is a state of mind that you choose to experience. It has nothing to do with outer experiences. Outer experience can amplify your experience of joy and happiness, but it is the choice that will set you free. Then you will not have to seek happiness because you will be creating joy instead.

Happiness is a byproduct of productive and happy thoughts. So your key to happiness lies in choosing wise and beneficial thoughts.

Thoughts are energy in creation, and this energy moves in the direction of your choices and beliefs.

So, my family and friends, don't look for happiness; rather, seek to monitor your thoughts, and as the quality of your thoughts improve, so will your life. And you will be happier.

Where do thoughts emanate from? Are they from an experience, or are they being drawn from the collective thought forms of humanity? Asking this question can set you free.

The highest thoughts come from your soul. When thoughts are produced from all three parts of you — body, mind, and soul — in full synchronicity, you will produce the highest possible outcome. This in turn will produce the highest joy and happiness in your life.

MASTER RUMI ON

Innocence

Innocence is the essence of life, indeed, for all are innocent, and nothing can be judged. Who are we to judge? You are a universe in creation, and a universe is never concluded and is ever expanding.

So judge not and condemn not, for you do not know a soul's path in this life or others. Seek innocence in everyone you see, and they will see the same within you. All are pure and innocent at the core level. They have merely forgotten while doing the things you call evil.

Stand still and breathe, and pull up this quality within you. Then you will start to see beauty and love flowing from others' hearts, and in this, you will see beauty and innocence in all.

God neither judges nor condemns, for God knows that you have merely forgotten who you are. God allows you in your innocence to heal and come back once again to the truth of who you are.

Innocence is the byproduct of your soul, for there are many qualities the soul has, and innocence is on the top of the list.

Say daily and loudly, "I am innocence and beauty, and these are the core essences I live by, moment to moment, in the eternal creation of me and in the magical moment of now.

"In this, I define myself and God within me. This is the message I send to the world, for my life is my message.

"If I were to die today, I would go with the knowledge and satisfaction that I lived by my truth of innocence and of love and laughter and that I glorified my God through these qualities.

"I am innocence and beauty and love."

MASTER RUMI'S

Tribute to Mothers

Mother, Mother, who are you?
Are you a goddess? Are you a god who creates and embodies?
Mother, Mother, who are you?
Are you a celestial being in human disguise, carrying on the work of Creator?
Mother, Mother, who are you?
Are you a being who embodies the spirits of earth and sky to show us the light and the way?
Mother, Mother, who are you?
Are you the Moon, the stars, and the galaxy we all gaze at with wonder?
O, my dear Mother, I honor you today, for you are the dear embodiment of all and more. I honor you for your love, caring, and giving and for the countless times you've loved me.
Even at times when I did not love you, you stood by me, knowing, "My child will return home." You knew that I'd return to your bosom.
You are an embodiment of pure and simple love, and I am overjoyed to be part of you and for coming through you.
I ask you to teach me this simple love you carry in your heart so that I can share this pure love with all who cross my path.
Be my teacher, be my mentor, be my guide, my dear mom, for this love of yours will light up the world and burn brightly long after you are gone.
This will be the gift you will leave to the world and me.

MASTER RUMI ON

Love

Love is a gift we are born with, and this gift is free to share. The more we share, the more it grows.

Then why do you restrict yourself in sharing this ever-present gift? What misery are you going through in your mind and life that you restrict its flow?

Don't you see that when it doesn't flow, it stagnates and rots? Do you want your magnificence to be like a lifeless corpse, or do you want to shine your light brightly and clearly?

Then love is the answer. Love. Love. Love.

This love has been expressed and shared through the teachings of the masters of yesteryear. It is expressed in your beautiful paintings, music, dance, fun, and laughter.

This love weaves the world together and holds humanity in its tenderness. This love consoles a broken heart or soothes a broken mind.

Your four-legged brothers and sisters display this love and share it freely always. Have you seen a mother bird feeding her little ones or a mama cat feeding her kittens? That is the purest form of love.

Seek a four-legged brother and sister, and look into its eyes. What will you see? Love staring back at you.

When you are down and out, look to your own beautiful eyes. You will see your love staring back at you.

You are love, love, love.

MASTER RUMI ON

The Love Within

Love is what it is. It has no name or color, for it is just as it is.
You can give it a name, and you can describe it, but does it need to be described, or would you rather feel it, be it? Do you do it justice in your description, or is it a figment of your imagination?
Seek not to love through need; rather, seek to share love through mutual cooperation.
Seek love not to possess but to release.
Seek love not to control but to be controlled by it.
Seek love not to be jealous but to heal the energy of jealousy within you.
Seek love not for self-gratification but to give love to others.
Seek love not for adulation but to show what love can do to unite people.
Seek love so that you can serve people and serve God, for they are the same.
Seek love to bring light and laughter to others — to all those whose lives you touch — for in this, you will glorify yourself and God, for you are God and love, indeed.
Seek love not outside yourself but within, for there is an eternal fountain of love inside you.
Quench your thirst from it, and you will be filled with it, for not only will it fill you up but you will also share this love freely with all.

You are the love, God, and universe combined as one, and it is called love.

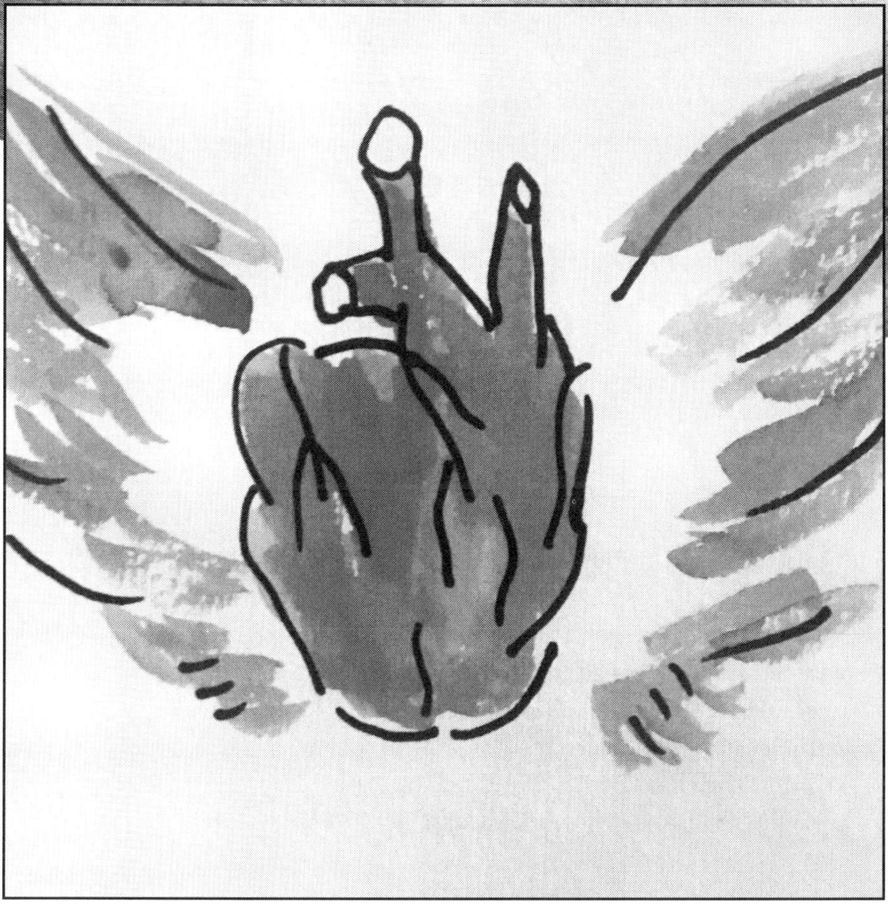

MASTER RUMI ON

The Love You Seek

Love is like the fragrance of a beautiful flower; it uplifts everyone who is around.

Love is simple and pure, for it does not have ego or need; it just is.

You are this love, and this love emanates its beautiful scent without opening its mouth to say anything. It just is.

You know this love full well, for you were created by it and sustained by it.

Seek this love, for it is embedded in your cells and skin. When you open it, you will never close it again, for it will nourish and sustain you. Your soul is fed by it, and it sings its glory in all its ways — through dance, song, and paintings.

You hear love's glory through the birds' singing, the bees' humming, the children's laughter, a loved one's gentle touch, or a lover's knowing glance.

You see this love in nature in all its glory. You see it in the velvety night sky with its shining stars and in the majestic mountains with their immense trees and rocks. You see this love as the dolphins and whales swim.

The entire cosmos dances to this love, for the cosmos is made of this love, and it is this love that sustains it and makes it grow forever forward.

Dance to this love, and you will dance to life.

MASTER RUMI ON

Love Is God

Love is the wind gently caressing your cheek and hair, never seen but always felt and touched, uplifting you.

But what is love?

People say it is a feeling, an emotion, or a thought. I say it is all this and more. I say

Love is silence.

Love is wisdom.

Love is action.

Love is divine timing.

I set out to practice the four virtues of love and wondered how love can be silence. In silence, I heard, "It is true."

I then wondered, "How is love wisdom?"

And in silence, I heard, "It is true, for in having wisdom, one expresses love in its many forms."

This, I understood, and I asked, "How is love an action?"

I heard, "It is in the expression of caring; through caring actions, love is expressed."

This, I fully grasped, and I wondered, "How is love in divine timing?"

I heard, "When we combine the first three attributes of love, then one is able to express it in the most appropriate and divine timing in the manner and form in which it will be most accepted and appreciated."

Then I wondered, "Are there Gods for love — one for human love and one for divine love?"

The answer was love itself, for love has another name. It is called God/Goddess.

MASTER RUMI ON

Marriage

What is Marriage? Is it a holy reunion, and if not, what it is?

Marriage is a rekindling of old souls coming together again to rejoice in the reunion of your soul. In this dance of life, through this reunion, you will discover more of who you are and who your partner is.

Therefore, seek not your holy partner to fulfill you. Rather, give space for your partner to grow and fulfill him- or herself, for you both are sacred divinity clothed in human bodies.

Seek not your partner to be in service of you but to be in service to others and to God. In this, you will fulfill the purpose of holy reunion.

You both have danced the life of man and woman many times through this universe and elsewhere. So in this dance in this lifetime, be the dancer and the dance. Be the music, dance, and merriment — all of it.

Should this end, be not in sorrow, for this was a dance. It was play, and all dances and play have beginnings and endings.

The dance between two souls never truly ends. It just takes on different forms, that's all. The soul seeks a new dance with a new rhythm and a new melody in each of its life forms.

So be in the moment of this sacred dance and holy reunion, for it can end in a flash. Do not possess it or be afraid to lose it. Instead, embrace it fully in the present moment of now.

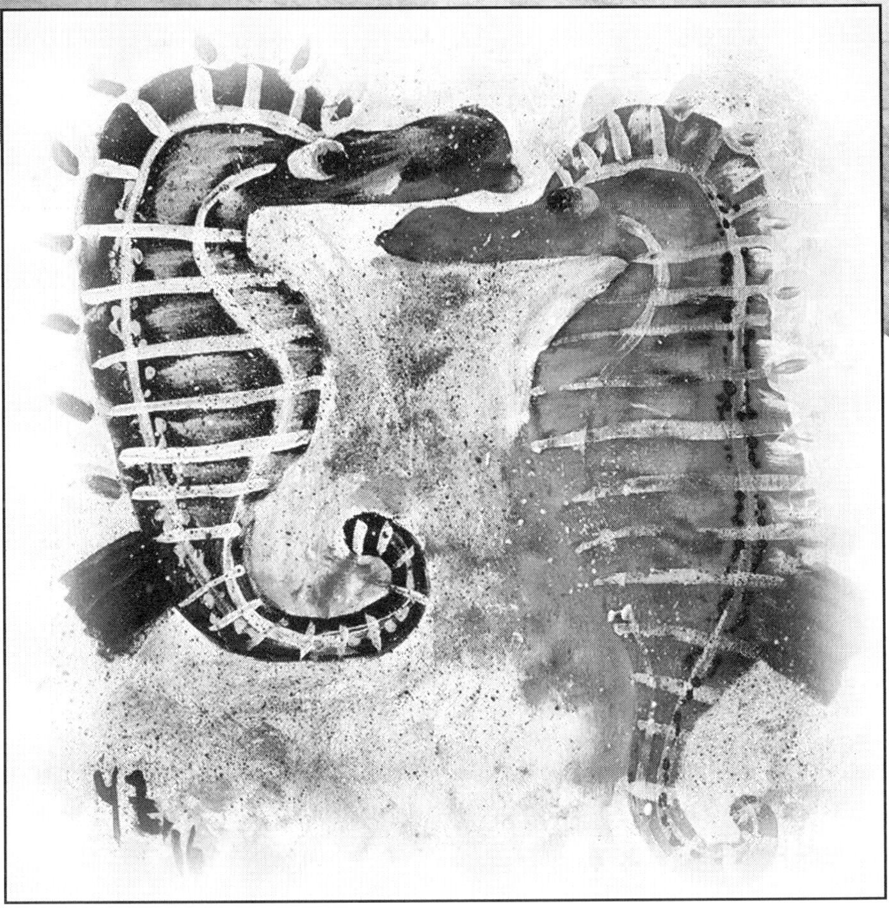

MASTER RUMI ON

Money

Money, money — everyone wants money, and they toil, fight, steal, and even kill for it.

But what is money other than a form of exchange? That is all there is to it, for money is not who you are or who you will ever be.

Enjoy and celebrate money, but never become it, for in becoming it, you will degrade your divinity and glory.

Money is simply a commodity to be shared freely and easily, not hoarded and hidden. The universe is abundant, and when you know this, you will loosen the grip on this corruptible energy.

You will know there is plenty for everyone and every time, and it never runs dry. In this, you will find freedom and liberation, for your whole life is geared toward making money.

From the time you are born, you are taught to be competitive and smart, and when you do this, you can become successful, and life will be rich with money and all other possessions.

In this process, you have taken away the innocence of the little ones, and they grow up in the belief that they have to fight and compete to get to the top, and they pass this on to their offspring. And the cycle continues.

Is there a way to stop this madness from fully enveloping the world?

The answer is yes, yes, yes! Stop being possessed by money. When you are possessed by it, you will become a slave to it.

See money as what it is — a means of exchange — and that is all. In this, you will find freedom.

Yes, you need to survive in this world, and for this, you need money. If you look at your life in the present moment, you will see that you have enough to survive and move into the next moment. You will notice that you always had everything to survive.

All else you thought you needed to survive was only an illusion. And this illusion came from your mind believing that you need something to survive.

Ponder this, brothers and sisters, and you will see the futility of the race to succeed and accumulate.

MASTER RUMI ON

The Seasons

Seasons are like colors on a palette, with many hues and sounds. With each passing day, a new silhouette is formed with the majestic beauty of the Earth. And in this wondrous beauty, nature dances once again to the rhythm of life itself.

Nature is God in beauty and action, and nature sings a beautiful lullaby. If you stand still, you can hear this beautiful melody, and you can sing along with it, for there is harmony and peace in it.

Be one with nature and earth, for there is much more than you are able to see and understand.

Nature is a grand orchestra in the ever-eternal moment of producing its heart-filling symphony so that all in its body can rejoice and dance to this holy music.

Seasons are like a lover's paradise where each moment is eternal and glorious and where time stands still. One can be in this stillness and know oneself and God within.

Seasons are the golden canvas where Mother Earth paints her gorgeous canvas with exquisite colors of the leaves and the sky, and each hue produces a scintillating aroma that uplifts one's hearts and soul.

So come on out to play with the changing seasons and be one with them. And join in the chorus of the holy melody produced by the changing seasons.

In summer, the canvas is mostly made of blue and white.

In autumn, the canvas is of brilliant soft orange and yellow.

In winter, the canvas is painted with soft gray and pale white.

In spring, the canvas comes alive with all colors and sounds of the universe.

Seasons are the playground of all the little ones, from the bees and butterflies to the dragonflies and the birds, for without the seasons, life would become monotonous and a drag.

So welcome the changing of season with your own dance and song, and you will celebrate in the creation of life itself by God.

MASTER RUMI ON

Silence and Solitude

Solitude is the divine place where you find your core and essence. It is also a place where you find peace and contentment.

Seek this place daily, for in this, you are communicating with your beloved self.

Your twin flame of love is only found in solitude and contemplation, for you all seek this twin flame at the deepest part of your beings.

All your life, you search for it, and everything you do is to find this true love of yours. You yearn for it and search for it far and wide.

This drives you in all you do, this reunion with your beloved. However, it can be found only in your silent contemplation and solitude.

Seek solitude not to run or hide from the world, nor as an escape route to bury your sorrows. Seek it to fulfill your heart, for in this solitude, there is the nectar of love, and it is ready to pour into your hands and soul to quench your thirst.

Seek solitude to commune with your beloved, for in this communion, you will find yourself and all of nature, and the universal melody will fill your heart.

Solitude offers peace and creativity as well as good health and cheerfulness.

Solitude is the way the Divine communes with you, for the Divine seeks to commune with you as much as you wish to commune with the Divine.

In solitude, you will hear the gentle whisper of the night sky, the symphony of the shooting star, the gigantic roar of the northern lights, and the heartbeat of Mother Earth. All are alive and waiting to sing to you the heavenly melody that will fill you.

In the silence of solitude, you think that there is no sound, but nature is sound itself, for you and the universe were created by the sound sung in silence.

Some of your inspired musicians know this, and they composed the famous song "The Sound of Silence."

So seek solitude and silence, and do not be afraid of it. It is your friend and a great benefactor. Seek it, and be with it to join the royal chorus of gods and goddesses.

MASTER RUMI ON

Sorrow

Sorrow is grief bottled up. Get it out, and cleanse it with love and forgiveness, for sorrow can drown you in misery and apathy. Then you end up playing the victim game.

Arise from your slumber, take the reins of your life, and move forward. If you wallow in sorrow, you will be drowned in it and in your self-pity.

Arise, brave ones, for you are warriors of light, and you've come here to fight the darkness of ignorance and delusion. Wear the mantle of truth and wisdom, for this exists in your heart.

Claim it, own it, and live it, for this is the way of the light warrior, the one who shows the way for others to follow.

So do not stay in your grief and sorrow; there is nothing you can achieve by being in it. It will only drain you of your vitality.

There is immense strength and courage inside you. Go deep within, and unearth these qualities that are part of your soul. Arise again like the Phoenix. Spread your mighty wings, and take to the magnificent sky, for you are dear and beautiful, and the world is waiting for your gift.

Arise, arise, my broken-hearted one. There is help if you ask.

Your soul is mighty indeed. It is imbued with all the qualities of God, so you cannot fail. Arise! Arise, my little one, and fly once again.

MASTER RUMI ON

The Soul

One day my heart asked me, "Who am I?"
I answered, "I am everything"
My heart asked, "What is everything?"
I answered, "All That Is."
My heart asked, "What does it mean?"
I answered, "You will know."
"What is that?" my heart asked.
I answered, "In stillness, you will know and discover."

I sat in stillness, and I heard the rain and the wind talking to me, so I asked them, "Who are you?"
They collectively answered, "We are you."
My mind could not comprehend this, so I asked again.
The response was, "Go within."
I asked, "How do I do that?"
The answer was the same, "Go within. Be still."

So I practiced stillness. Then not only the rain and the wind spoke to me but also all of creation.
Then I realized that I was the creation, and I was talking to myself the whole time.

I am Yod and Vae.
I am Shiva and Shakti.
I am the Son, the Father, and the Holy Ghost.
I am the soul, the monad, and I am presence.

I Am That I Am. I Will Be That I Am. I Shall Be That I Am.
I am all of creation and the created, for I am pure energy.
I am the emptiness from which all creation comes forth.
I am the primordial force.
I am the clay that is used to manifest all.
I am all of it — the beginning and the end and the eternality of it.

I am. I am. I am. Soul.

MASTER RUMI ON

The Night Sky

One day in my childlike innocence and wonder, I looked up at the night sky and asked, "What is up there beyond the clouds, beyond the stars, and beyond and beyond?"

My heart gently whispered, "It is you, my little one. You are this vastness, beyond and beyond."

I asked, "What is beyond that?"

The answer was, "You and me and God."

I asked, "Who is God?"

My heart gently whispered, "It is you, others, and everything combined in wholeness."

Then I asked, "If I Am All That Is, how can I experience that?"

My heart gently answered, "In stillness, you will experience this and more."

I asked, "What is that?"

The answer was, "That which is not and that which was not."

I asked, "Is this the place I came from?"

The answer was, "From that which is not and that which was not, you were birthed."

Then I asked, "Where am I going?"

My heart gently answered, "You are going Home."

I asked, "Where is my Home?"

My heart whispered in response, "In love, you will discover and experience Home."

I longed for this Home of mine, and I knew that it was within me. I made it my mission to find and be in my Home for eternity. When I made this request from the fullness of my being, the doors of my Home swung open gently and invited me to enter.

I have been there ever since.

Everyone has a Home within. Go find it, for it is a place of goodness and plenty — plenty in peace, joy, and love. In this knowing, you will celebrate the Creator who birthed you from his loving heart.

I invite all of you to journey into your Home, for once you find it, you will never want to leave it. All your lives have prepared you for the moment when you will return Home.

MASTER RUMI ON

Infinity

Infinity is your true essence — a being without a beginning and an end in the endless cycles of different expressions of life, manifesting in various forms on Earth and with the stars.

You are the formless and indescribable one, for you are infinite, and infinity cannot be explained. It only can be felt within you.

In the continuum of life, some moments might seem like an eternity, and time can seem as if it is standing still, but in reality, you are moving and growing.

It's much like the bamboo that does not seem to be growing, and then with the invisible rays of the stars and the Sun, it grows tall and healthy.

Since you are infinite, your growth is assured as long as you get out of your own way and allow the natural process to take place.

The universe and everything else in it grows naturally, following each perfected plan in the bosom of its creation, and like a graceful dancer following the melody, your life will unfold in its eternity when you allow it.

Eternity is not what you seek, for it is you. You seek expressions of yourself in this eternal now moment. In this, you will experience the grander part of yourself — the divine part of you — and you will become one with the universe.

The universe is you, and everything you see is part of your eternal existence. The stars you see in the night sky, the Sun, the Moon, the planets orbiting the Sun — they are all part of your eternal existence.

Being fully in the present moment will help you experience glimpses of this eternality, and when you combine it with your silence and meditation, you will live in this eternal moment.

This is where you will fully find yourself.

This is where the worshipped and the worshipper become one.

Sneha Tali Mali Om.

MASTER RUMI ON

Enlightenment

A sudden jolt bolted me out of my deep slumber. I opened my eyes wide in disgust and fear. I wondered what shook me from my deep sleep, and then I saw a being standing at the foot of my bed with a gentle-looking face and a smile like the most innocent child.

The being asked me, "My child, come with me, for we are waiting. You have been here for a long time to remember and come back Home."

In my stupor, I felt like I was in a dream, and in the dream, I followed the being without knowing where I was going.

I kept walking, and I was led into a vast mansion with many chambers. I asked the being, "Who are you?"

The being answered, "I am your guide, and I have been with you, watching you and guiding you over your many life journeys, through all time and space."

I stood in awe, wondering how I could not have noticed my guide before. And before the question could be spoken, my guide answered, "Do not admonish yourself. The past does not matter, for you are in the process of creating a grand future."

I asked, "What are these chambers for?"

My guide answered, "They are yours to enter, and they are the chambers of peace, abundance, creativity, wisdom, strength, and courage."

I asked, "Who placed them there?"

I was answered, "You did."

Humbly, I entered each chamber and was engulfed by the most blessed feeling I ever had. Each chamber filled me with the memories of my soul and heart. I wept in remembrance of me.

I asked the being who showed me these chambers, "Can I take the essence of these back with me?"

I was told, "All is yours for the taking."

I gathered as many essences from these chambers as I could. With each essence, I felt heavier and heavier, and I wondered why.

My thought was answered, "You are not able to carry it because you are already full, and there is no space for any new things."

So for me to carry these beautiful essences, I will have to empty all that I know and believe in and adjust my thoughts and emotions to heal my wounds and forgive those whom I felt harmed me.

Then I have to bathe in the pure light of love and adorn my new clothes in divinity.

I felt this to be a heavy burden, and I asked, "Is there a simpler way for me to embody these essences?"

I was told, "Wisdom erases and balances all energy."

I understood and decided to discard all that did not serve me any longer. After I did this, effortlessly and easily the full essences of the chambers filled me, and I wept with joy and gratitude.

The being then said, "Now it is yours. Share it freely and abundantly, and your cup will never run dry, for now you carry the essence of one who created this all — you and God."

MASTER RUMI ON

Lovers

I looked into my beloved's eyes and said, "How beautiful and magnificent you are, for I see the beauty in your eyes and smell your sweet fragrance."

My lover looked into my eyes, holding my hands, and whispered, "You are beautiful too."

But I could not see it, and in my denial, I lost my senses and connection to myself.

My lover whispered, "You are magnificent."

I stood soaking it all in, and then I looked up at the night sky. The stars were shining on us with a loving intensity. Then I saw a shooting star sending a message that what my lover said was true indeed.

I felt the stirrings in my heart magnify, and I held my beloved in my arms. I kissed her tender and sensuous lips, and I caressed her tender breasts. I drank the love she offered me from her full cup. I was in ecstasy, for I was making love to my beloved.

I danced in the sacredness of this holy union, for it was a moment in eternity. The Moon looked at us and winked, and the stars celebrated. The universe sang its holy melody and rejoiced, for I have joined in this ecstasy of union with my beloved self.

I call this beloved self my holy divine.

MASTER RUMI ON

Friendship

Friendships are the bridges on which you can easily cross the troubled waters of life. A true friend is someone who is not only there for you in times of good and bad but who is there to point out and remind you who you truly are.

True friends see your soul, not just your body and personality. They neither judge nor condemn, for they know you are a work in progress and an ever-growing entity.

Treasure your good friends, and discard those who are vain and only looking for a shoulder to lean on, draining you and themselves.

Seek your friendships not to fill your emptiness but to share your fullness, and you will gain more.

In the world of duality you live in, you will come across many types of friends. Some will be in human form, and some will be other life forms. Do not discard any, for there can be friendship and growth among human beings, four-legged creatures, and all nature.

In friendship, you grow and your heart expands. In this expansiveness, you learn to experience love in its fullest, for when there is no love within for yourself or anybody else, then you can turn into a monster.

Cultivate this love through your friends and your soul, for they are the same in varying degrees.

In the waking of the soul, you will find your soul friends with whom you have shared much past — as in past realities. In this reunion in this lifetime, you will awaken the abundant love you had for each other that will fulfill a part of your divine destiny.

Friendships nourish not only your soul but also your entire well-being.

In waking up the divinity within you through deep friendship, the grass is nourished under your feet, and Earth is uplifted, for you are a dear friend to Mother Earth. You have come here to nourish and support her through your friendship and love.

MASTER RUMI ON

Parting

In the midst of my sorrow, I lifted my head and peeked into the darkness, into the emptiness, and I begged for release and freedom, for my heart ached so much.

Tears flowed in endless streams, and I clutched for a ray of hope to be reassured that this too shall pass. But in my mind, I saw only an abyss, and I wondered, "Why did he leave me so abruptly? Did I slight him or hurt him that he had to take leave of me?"

In my despair, I conjured all the scenarios and played them again and again in my heart. My tormented heart sang a song of deep despair, and I felt as though nature were weeping with me — the trees, the plants, the flowers, and all of it, for he was my bosom friend and lover. He was a friend to all.

Nature and everything agonized in his parting.

In my anguish, I cried out with folded hands to my God, who I know and worship, begging and pleading to bring my lover back.

My God just stared at me, mute. I pleaded with him and asked him again. I promised that I would do anything to get him back, and again there was no answer, only silence.

In my torment and sorrow, sleep seemed a welcome relief. I gently closed my eyes and fell into a deep state. Then my beloved appeared in a dream and whispered in my ear, "I am with you always. I have never left you. I cannot leave you, for you and I are joined in this eternal dance of life, death, and rebirth.

"So rejoice, my beloved. I shall be with you again and again. And your every thought and word shall reach me at the speed of light, for we are one, always."

MASTER RUMI ON

Death

Death is the great consoler.
Death is the great liberator.
Death is freedom.
Death is reunion.
Death is going Home.
Death is comforting.
Death is rejoining and remembering.

There is no death, only parting of certain ways and experiences. When you decide it is time to go, to create and play in another landscape, you leave your body and say goodbye.

Only in doing so can you create a new play with new actors and some old actors — all in a new setting. You are in the eternal process of self-discovery and expansion.

So do not grieve death. Celebrate in the return!

In grieving those who have left the body, you deny them forward movement, and you are only fulfilling a part of your ego. When you do not let go, you hold them back from their journeys.

You do so to fulfill your agenda, not theirs. So let them go, knowing that they have chosen to exit now.

Death is a mystery, for in not knowing what death is, you wallow in sorrow. Death is a doorway to another reality, and what you carry through this doorway when you exit creates your reality in the new arena.

So prepare for your death every day, for it can occur any moment. The big question is, "What are you carrying back when you exit?"

Welcome Death with open arms, just as you welcome birth.

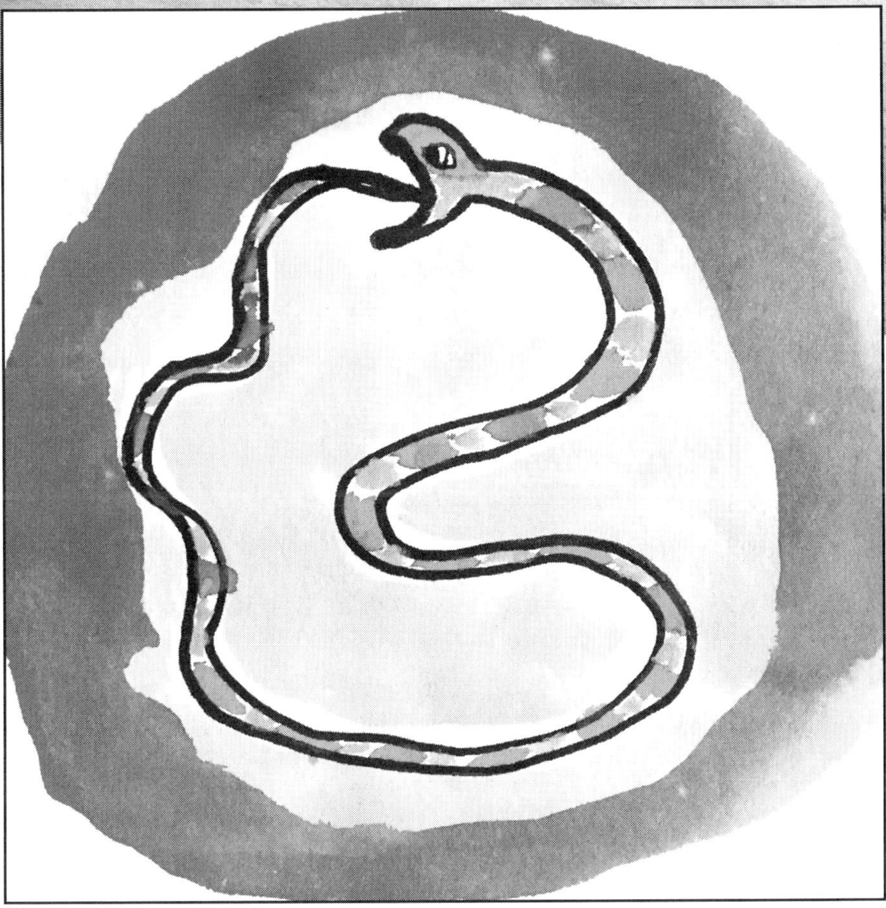

MASTER RUMI ON

Teachers

Teach. Teach. Teach. In teaching, you learn about yourself. That is the purpose of teaching.

In teaching, you know yourself, and in knowing yourself, you express yourself fully. In this expression, you rediscover yourself, and the circle is complete. The teacher and the student become one.

Teachers join the hearts and minds of their students and all humanity, but first they must join their own. This they demonstrate moment by moment through their expressions of life and love, and in those expressions, they exhibit their mastery.

You all have come to master your lives and be sources for others to master their lives too. So do not withhold your wisdom, because by doing so, you would break an ancient code that says, "With those who come sincerely, I will share all that I know."

When shutting out sharing, you deny yourself, for there are no others but you.

Share your knowledge, wisdom, and love with all, for all are parts of you. Never deny a parched soul seeking truth, for you will be committing a grave injustice.

Have not the wise elders shared with you all the truths they have discovered and experienced? And in this sharing, they have elevated themselves and others and earth spirit.

I ask all teachers to share their wisdom, for only in sharing, can you be called teachers and masters.

There are many lost souls seeking freedom; seek them, and share freely. Do not be in your ego mind or shut out those who come, cursing them and casting them away. In doing so, you would devolve to their status.

Do not sit on a golden throne, and do not be in the glory of it all, in the ill-mannered worship and devotion of a sleeping humanity. Instead, rise above it, and be a gentle soul.

Mingle and be with all just as they are, and in doing so, you will exhibit your mastery in teaching.

MASTER RUMI ON

Tears

Tears, tears, tears — what are they? Are they an indication of sorrow or something else?

Tears are the purifying balm of your soul, for in crying, you cleanse and purify your heart and soul. You nourish your soul, and the trueness of you is revealed.

So do not say no to tears. Welcome them. Embrace them, for tears are a healing balm and nurturing energy.

Tears can wipe away your sins.

Tears can heal and forgive.

Tears can unite you to become strong once again.

Tears can ignite long-lost dreams.

Tears can bring hope and love into your life.

There are many kinds of tears. There are tears of sadness, tears of joy and laughter, tears of remembrance, and tears of forgiveness and reconciliation.

All tears originate from the heart, and they should be released and not held tight, for in releasing them, you will find freedom and joy.

Tears break open hardened hearts and minds so that truth and compassion can seep in. Tears water a parched soul. If allowed to flow freely, tears will lead you into your own garden where you will discover your inner beauty.

So take the time to allow tears once a week or once a month. Make it an exercise in self-discovery.

In remembering past hurts and sorrows, and through sharing and tearing, you will release deep-seated emotions to make space for healing and love to enter.

I welcome you to do so, and I will be with you.

MASTER RUMI ON

Devotion

Devotion is who you are, and who you are is God. You have forgotten this, and you only need to remember it.

In this remembrance, you will embrace your divinity. In this, you will build the courage to accept and have faith in yourself.

In accepting yourself fully now and not looking at the past but at who you could be from this moment on, you will create the new you. This is divinity in action.

Divinity is also when you are divine with others and to nature and to all, for then you see only divinity in all, and you express this through your words and actions, and you become one with the divine you interact with.

Divinity is when you see beauty in others.

Divinity is when you comfort another.

Divinity is when you smile and laugh with another.

Divinity is when you forgive others.

Divinity is when you express and experience compassion with others.

Divinity is when you honor another.

Divinity is when you uplift another.

Divinity is when you share with another freely.

Divinity is when you give hope to another.

Divinity is when you love another without condition.

Divinity is when you bring wisdom to others.

Divinity is when you accept another.

Divinity is when you choose to see only the bright and positive side in another.

Divinity is when you can say honestly, "I am true to myself. I am true to myself and God within me. I am true to myself, God, and the universe within me."

Divinity is when you are true to yourself.

Divinity is when you are truthful to yourself and others.

Divinity is when you express joy to yourself and others.

Divinity is when you sing and dance to the grand rhythms of life.

Divinity is when you are playful like a child.

Divinity is when you stand in your inner courage and trust yourself.

Divinity is when you can freely share your body and your life, knowing fully that you are eternal and you are divine.

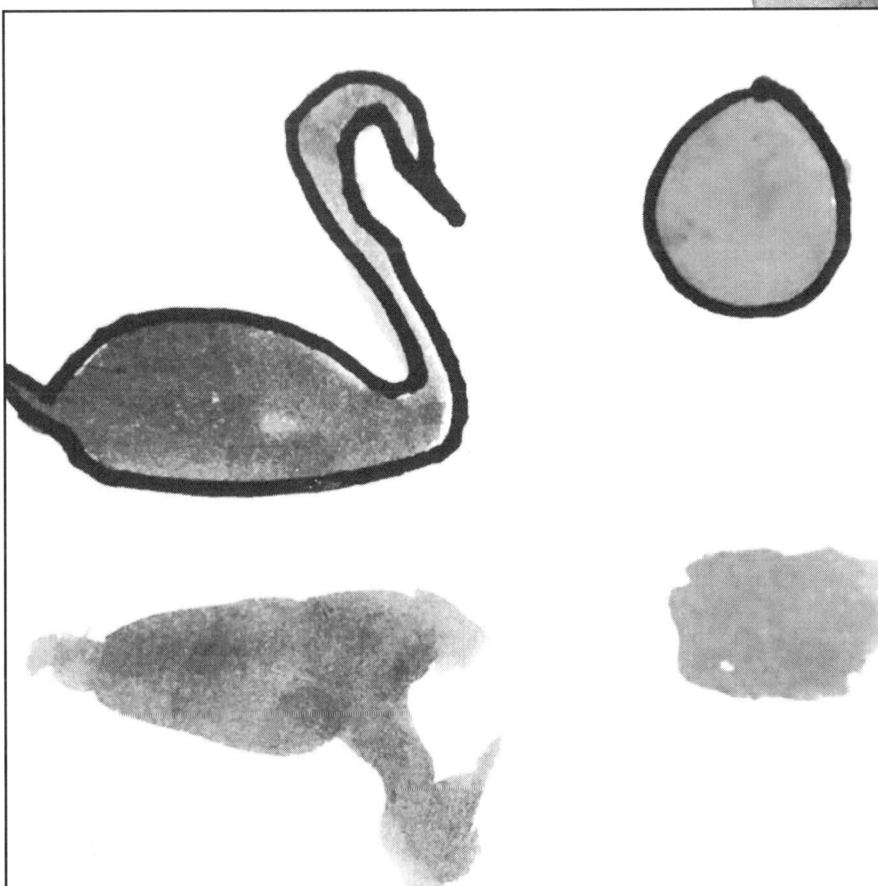

MASTER RUMI ON

Dreams

"Dreams, dreams, dreams — what are they?" I wonder. These cross my mind without rules or patterns, and I wonder what they are all about, where they come from, and where they go.

So I set out to solve this mystery, as I have heard others wonder the same thing, "What do dreams mean?"

Like a warrior dressing in battle gear, I put on in my foolish ego-based knowledge, and said aloud, "I am going to find out what dreams are all about, and I am going to tell all. All will rejoice in this knowingness and be free of these incoherent images and thoughts that cross their minds during sleep time."

When I took the first step in this magical land to find the source of my dreams, I was told, "Drop your battle gear." I reluctantly let go of what I had known or read about dreams.

Then I was asked to empty my mind. And this I did to the best of my ability.

Next, I was escorted into the dream factory where all dreams are created and sent forth.

It was a magical land, indeed, with many beings poring over charts, diagrams, and blueprints — looking over many codes and numbers. They were all busy.

I asked one of them, "What is this place?"

I was told that I was witnessing the creation of dreams, and these dreams would be sent forth into people's subconscious minds while they sleep.

Each dream has a meaning and great substance to it, and those who know how to decode it will be great masters, for dreams are teachers. They are here to support us in our daily lives.

I took it all in and was amazed at the beauty and the intricate network through which dreams are created to support us. I asked, "Who created all this?"

I was told, "It was created by you, along with your supporting energies."

Then I understood, and before I left, I asked one final question: "Can I use it to find myself and love myself with my dreams?"

And I got the answer, "Yes."

When I came back, I talked to the spirit of dreams, and I asked to be shown how to know, experience, and love myself fully. I was asked to talk to the spirit before I went to sleep and to request that the dreams to be programmed into making what I want to create.

I started doing this, which started creating magic and miracles in my life. I invite you to do so too.

MASTER RUMI ON

The Garden

In the garden of my heart, I realized there is eternal beauty, and I set out to find it, but I could not see it. It seemed as if it were evading me even though its fragrance filled my senses.

I wondered, "Will I ever find my inner garden?" I kept looking, knowing that if I did so, I would find it.

I looked harder and harder, but it always seemed to evade me. In my frustration and anger, I cried aloud: "I give up! I give up! I give up!"

I sat in silence and agony, feeling like a failure, and I started to cry. Tears rolled down my cheeks, and as I tasted the salt in my tears, I closed my eyes and lay down.

Then I dreamed, and in the dream, I was running around. I met a wise man on the street, and I asked him, "How can I find the flowers of my garden and my eternal beauty?

He said that he did not know. He told me to go ask the trees.

I ran to the trees and asked the same question, and the trees told me to go within to find it.

I said, "I did, but I did not find my garden," and the tree told me to go back and look deep within and ask for it to be revealed.

I did as the tree guided, and what did I find? The most beautiful garden sparkling with the jewels of my heart.

Each jewel sparkled beautifully in varying colors, creating a magnificent kaleidoscope.

I asked, "Is that me?"

The garden answered, "Yes, it is you. You have been there for eternity."

I understood, and in this understanding, I embraced myself fully.

I realized that I am the garden and everything in it. I am eternity, and I am all of it.

MASTER RUMI ON

Home

The Home is where I came from; the Home is where I return.
I wondered aloud, "What is Home?"
I heard, "Home is where the heart and love exist."
I asked, "Does my home have a name?"
The answer was, "God."
Now I know my home is my God and God is my home. In this knowingness, I sat in silence and contemplation. I noticed that my home was not a place but a feeling, an inner knowing. I wondered, "How much time I can spend in my home, in my knowingness?"
The answer was, "Forever, for eternity."
I heard a voice say, "In staying for eternity, you would not know what eternity or God means, for there will be nothing other than Eternity/God."
So I asked, "To know Eternity/God/Home, do I need to step out of my home?"
The answer came, "Yes, for only in the relative you can know the absolute."
I paused to wonder, and I realized that in the absence of anything, I cannot experience the other, and I realized the true meaning of yin and yang within me.
I realized my Home is made up of me/the me — as a man and as a woman.
Now I know I am neither man nor woman.
I am Eternal Being.
I am Pure Form.
This is my eternal Home, where I return again and again.

MASTER RUMI ON

The Rose

Rose said to itself, "I am beauty and beautiful."

Rose looked at its neighboring flower and said, "It is as beautiful as I am."

She looked over to the other side of the garden, and those flowers in the garden were beautiful too. Then she went to the edge of the garden, and all the flowers there were beautiful too.

Rose wondered, "Is everything as beautiful as me?" And her heart answered, "Yes, yes, yes."

Then Rose asked her spirit, "Who and what created this beauty?"

The answer was pure and simple. Her spirit whispered, "It was created by love."

Now Rose understood, and she asked whether she could share her beauty and love with others so that they could see their own beauty and love.

Her Spirit responded with a resounding yes.

That is how the rose was chosen to be the symbol of love.

Then I heard the heart whisper again, and this time it was profound:

"You are love.

"We are love.

"They are love.

"You and I breathe love."

Love to live.
Live to love.
Love to be.

MASTER RUMI ON

The Heart & Mind

Like the bow and string are both needed to play beautiful music on a violin, I realized that my heart and mind are both needed for me to play my beautiful music on Earth.

In my search for myself, I had discarded my mind fully, believing in someone's teachings that only when you discard your mind can you know yourself and go to the place I was going to.

Now I realize that on my journey, my heart led me only in one way; however, when I combined it with my mind, I realized that I could go in many ways.

I realized that I need both on my journey, so I wholeheartedly embraced my mind and my heart. When I did this, true magic began to happen: I realized that my mind was also deeply divine and holy, just as my heart was.

When I use it in mindfulness, I can create divine experiences, and from these divine experiences, all experiences are created.

My prayer for today is

"My mind is pure and holy, and my holy mind produces divine and pure thoughts. From these pure thoughts are created pure energy, and from this pure energy, I create and experience who I am."

Embracing Divine Mind = Embracing Pure Creation Energy = Manifestation

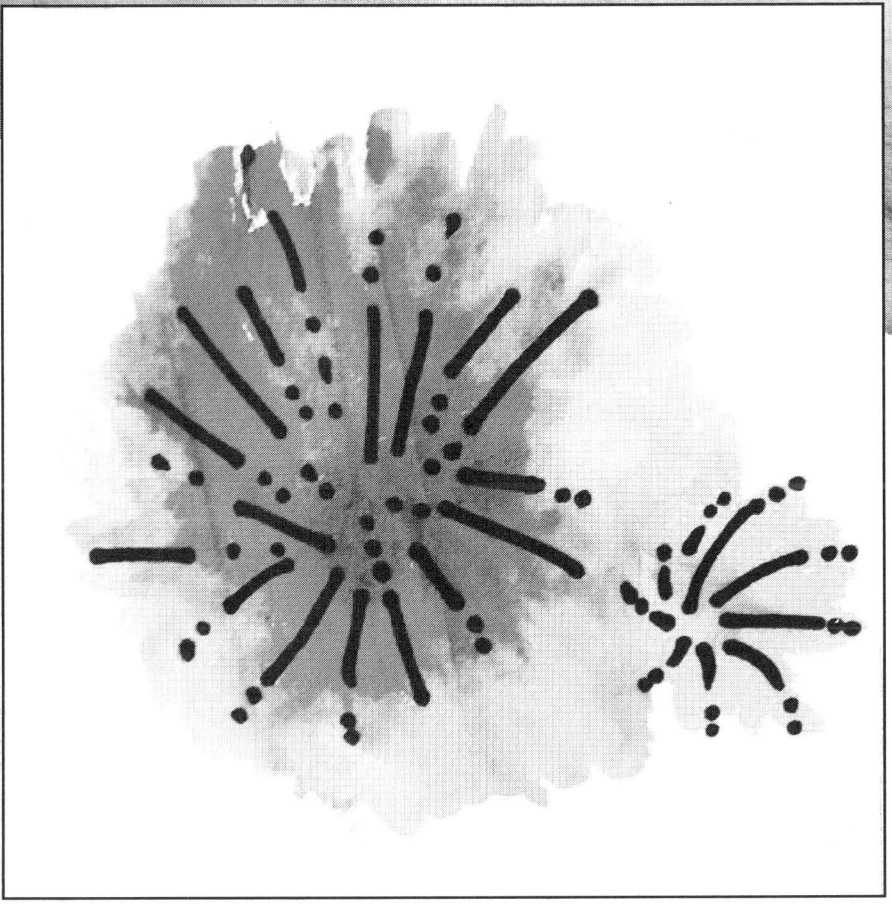

MASTER RUMI ON

My Beloved

As the waves of the ocean wash the shores, bringing all that needs to be left ashore, my soul brings out all that needs to be released. But in my ignorance, I grieve at my loss without knowing what I am letting go of. It is only my attachment and has no true value.

Experience can ever leave me.

Now I am washed clean of the sludge and mud I had carried for long. I am now fully dressed in my finest garment to meet my beloved, whom I have read about and heard about from others but never fully experienced.

I jump in ecstasy and excitement, knowing full well that my beloved has always been me. I had simply forgotten with the heavy weight of forgetfulness that I had carried.

I know and will never let go of my beloved, for my beloved is me, me, me.

My beloved is divine.

My beloved is sacred and supreme.

My beloved is beauty.

My beloved is peace, freedom, and joy.

My beloved is wisdom.

My beloved is the stars, the Sun, and the Moon; the trees, rocks, stones, and minerals; the rivers and the mountains; and All That Is.

My beloved is omnipotent.

My beloved is omnipresence.

My beloved is the vast emptiness.

My beloved is God in individuation.

MASTER RUMI ON

Children

Children are God in disguise, clothed in small bodies. Their presence in your life uplifts you and encourages you to be like them again, for in their innocence, they display the qualities of God — of love, laughter, and full self-expression in the moment of now.

Honor children, for they have chosen you to be their blessed parents, and in their knowing, they have willingly come into your home and lives, for they are master teachers and great thinkers.

Children are many and varied, and they come from afar — from the outer space, the farthest reaches of the universe — bringing with them special and unique gifts and talents.

Wise are the parents who are there for the children in their growing years.

Make them your friends and hold them in respect, and they will, in return, do the same for you and others, for they are wise beyond their years.

Children have come here carrying a heavy burden: the burden to lift the darkness from Earth. And this they will do through their inner knowing and new ideas.

So make way for them and support them along their paths, for they are the peacemakers of tomorrow. The new ones do not carry the past imprint of their fathers and other ancients, for they have come with clean slates and clean minds.

Give them the space to be who they are, and they will bloom like beautiful flowers. Each petal of the flowers will carry a new blueprint for the awakening humanity.

Honor the children; honor them, for they are tomorrow's adults. In nurturing them, you will heal your own wounds, and your inner child will make peace within you.

Welcome children into your life and home, for they are bundles of joy, laughter, and mischief. Being with them, you will forget your worries and sorrow if only for a moment, and you will again discover hope in your heart.

MASTER RUMI ON

The Beauty of Animals

Animals and birds are the angels sent by God to support human beings. When you look into their eyes, what do you see? God/the Universe. They are the children of God come here to brighten and support humanity, for they know they can be anchors for the sleeping humanity, and through their love, humanity will once again awaken from deep slumber.

In their eagerness to help the sleeping humanity, the animals gave up the comfort of their homes and families. They volunteered to come here knowing full well that they would be scorned and lynched by the sleeping humans, but their love was so great that they said, "We will volunteer to go to Earth."

A call was put out by the Creator for all to come, and they came to support all of us. So honor the animals for who they are — beautiful, kindred souls in service to humanity and Earth.

Earth is a paradise with a variety of animals — beauties. Animals enhance Earth's beauty with their divine presence. Have you ever stood still and watched the exquisite dance of the peacock or the prancing of little kittens? What do you see? Innocence and beauty all rolled into individual packages.

All creation is here to support you in your journey of self-discovery. When you acknowledge it — make it your truth — you will sing the animals' praises and be wowed by their tenderness and lightheartedness.

You will be rekindled, your tenderness and innocence, and then the circle will be complete.

Animals are the teachers of humanity in the gentlest way. Observe them to see how they interact, how they share with one another, and how they create communities in which their young ones can grow.

Listen to the animals' songs, and watch them play, for there is meaning in that.

They are modeling a different lifestyle for you to emulate. In this, you will find peace, joy, and harmony.

The little winged ones that you call butterflies, are they not magnificent and delicate in their exquisite colors? They spread the original energy of love that was seeded into the planet before human beings ever set foot on this Earth.

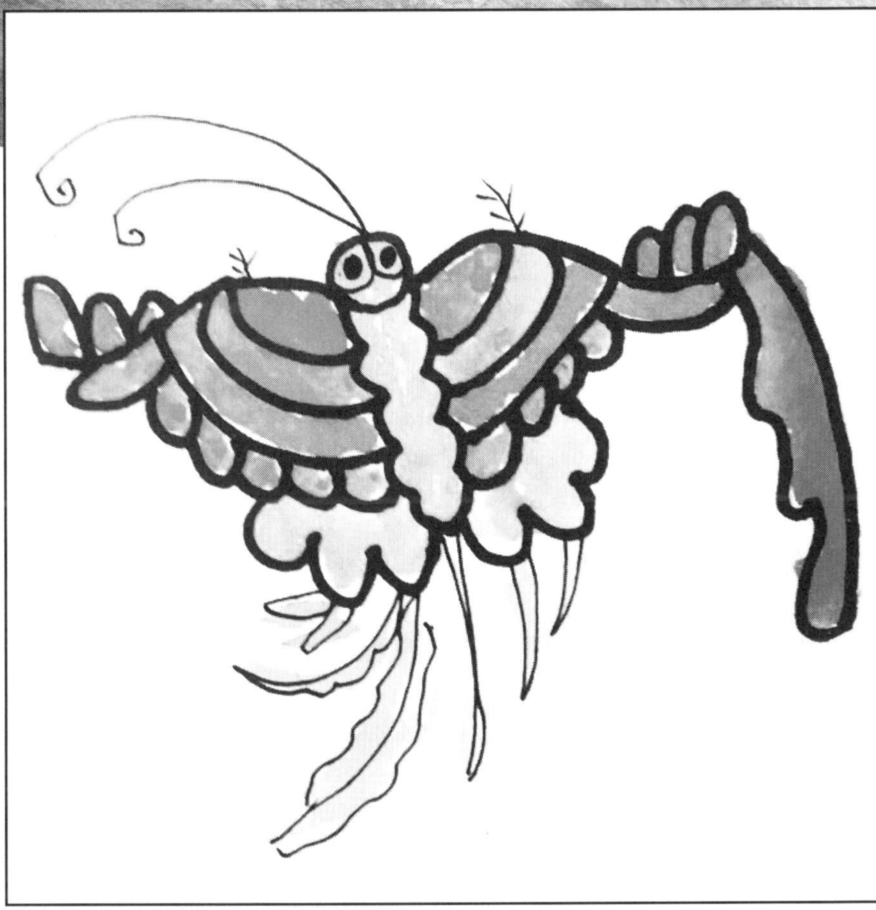

Observe the little one you call Bambi, and you will see, pure beauty in the purest form of love, for these two beings — the butterfly and the Bambi — were two of the first beings to come to the planet.

Honor all, for they are the master teachers of values and sharing. When you observe them, you will see that they do not take more than they need, and they only take what they put in. Hence, the circle of life is complete.

MASTER RUMI ON

Self-Realization

Like a snake shedding its skin, I decided this moment to shed my old, for my old was contracting me, binding me, and limiting me. I decided today that this house I've lived in does not support me anymore in who I want to be. It has become a prison cell and not a place of joy and freedom.

I decided to seek greener pastures, so I stepped out into the void, and there was darkness. Oh boy, was I scared.

I was tested and stripped naked of all things I thought belonged to me — my treasured possessions collected over many lifetimes, things I held dearly.

I stood alone, shivering in this darkness, devoid of all my possessions, and I realized that in this new land, I cannot carry my old baggage. I must travel lightly.

I continued shedding the remnants of my past that I still carried within me. A voice inside me told me to search deep in my being for what I still held on to and had not yet released.

I looked deep and found that I was carrying the energies of expectations, and the voice told me to release them.

I cried out, "Noooo," because this was the last thread reminding me of my identity. Then I saw a sign in front of me: "No Admittance with Old Baggage."

I reluctantly let go of my expectations, and I shivered, thinking about what was on the other side of the gate. I was afraid of the unknown. My legs were paralyzed with fear.

Then I heard a commanding voice tell me, "Move!" And as if a force had pushed me, I moved in front of the gate. Then I cut all the remnants of any residual energy still within me.

Like magic, the gates flew open, and I heard a little voice ask, "Why have you come, Holy One? What brought you here, Holy One?"

I answered, "I have come to join with the holiness that I am and to wear the crown of my truth and glory once again."

I heard the voice respond, "You may now enter, Holy One."

I saw a path in front of me. I was in a sacred place. As I walked on the path, I felt lighter and lighter. I noticed that this path had many crisscrossing roads, many overpasses, and it was leading me somewhere. In this knowingness, I walked on.

This path was leading me into my heart, and this time, I was clothed in the new me.

My heart, my heart;
My home, my home;
My sweet home, my sweet home;
My eternal Home.

MASTER RUMI ON

Moon

The Moon beams on me in the nighttime, and in my delusion, I believe that the Moon is only active in the nighttime.

But now I am awake, and I know that the Moon is always active and there is no night and day. In the same way, we drift from delirium to wakefulness only to fall asleep once again.

Now I rub my eyes and keep them open, knowing that the light and the shadow that I am are reflections of my imagination.

I am neither light nor its opposite, for I am the formless one — the eternal, ever-changing one.

I am thee.

I am God.

I am Goddess.

I Am.

MASTER RUMI ON

Family

What is a family? Is it a collection of people, or is it something larger?

What is the meaning of family? Are they to support one another or enhance and share with one another?

Your family is who you are, for all the people in your family, you have called on, and you have known them all along — not only in this lifetime, but over several times.

Each changes and sometimes reverses the roles, for you wanted to experience all of it — being a father, a mother, an uncle, a grandpa, a girl, an elder brother, all of it. So you asked everybody in your family to come together in this lifetime to play, balance, love, discover, and create more of your experience.

Honor your family, all of them.

Yes, sometimes they are the tough taskmasters, and sometimes they are the ones who give you the deepest pain and cause you great sorrow, for in rebalancing and linking between each other, all of you awaken the love quotient within.

This love may touch them, those who give you grief, for they would have forgotten who they are while causing you grief and sorrow.

Through your love, they will awaken, and your entire family will be healed. This is the purpose of family: to celebrate, sing, dance, and re-calibrate the grand love one has for another.

In this, you celebrate God, the Creator within you.

MASTER RUMI ON

Kundalini

The life force you are born with and carry within you, the key to opening your inner door, has been unused for a long time, and the locks are rusted and dirty. Now the key needs to be polished, and the door kept open, for in this New Earth, it is imperative that you awaken to your truth.

Be your own guide and teacher, and discard all that does not support making yourself anew. This you vowed when you were born.

You will use this life stream to awaken and open this atomic power within you to claim your magnificence so that you and the gods become one.

In the stillness of your heart, make a request for this power to reveal itself, and the coil of kundalini will stir from its long sleep and begin its upward movement through your spinal column, igniting the fire of love and wisdom so that you can live your life as a master and a humble servant.

Arise, arise kundalini! It is the primordial force within you. Sing to it. Talk to it. Make it your best friend, for who can be a better friend than your soul?

Your soul is the superstar of your entire being, and it sings and blends its beautiful harmony with the grand orchestra of the world.

Arise, arise, divine mother kundalini, for you are a goddess in divinity and devotion! There is love and compassion within you and courage and strength to be the leader once again of the ignorant masses who have been sleeping for eons.

O merciful one, the Shakti within me, I bow and surrender to you, for your embrace gently caresses my soul and heart.

I once again believe in myself, my goodness, and in the world I live in.

I long to be with you, kundalini Shakti, and become an eternal being, to dance on the stars and the sky and on the Earth plane without the shadow of illusion following me day and night.

I created this shadow to dance and self-realize, and now since I am awakened, I set this shadow aside and see the truth in all, for you have opened my eyes to my inner truth, and I will never close it again.

O Mother of all, I bow and honor you! Your immense strength now acts like a strong beacon of light in this dark world. Now I carry this truth and wisdom, and it will be my new walking stick.

I embrace all with the love and sacredness of my heart, and we become one. Lovers have joined lovers, and all have become whole again, neither man nor woman but rather a being of fullness.

MASTER RUMI ON

Shadows

People sometimes ask what shadows are. Are they reflections of you or something larger? Is there a greater meaning in shadows?

I say to you, shadows speak. Look for the shadows, and you will discover their secret beauty.

Like a diamond that is hidden in the mud and silt, your shadow self offers you glimpses of life's mysteries veiled in a thin disguise of illusion and forgetfulness.

Embrace the shadows, for you are casting a great treasure. When creating you, light cannot exist without the shadow. Both are complementary, and both have a purpose.

Look at the young ones. They embrace their shadows fully, and they laugh with them and cry with them, for they own them. By doing this, they heal.

Shadows are the harbingers of truth and change, for without shadows, you would not know what the full truth is.

So seek the shadow. Embrace it. Ask it to reveal its secret, and you will discover your hidden gems.

Shadows are not gray and dark. They are your subtle qualities that are to be embraced and healed. When you do this, you will know your true nature, and your true nature is God.

Seek this God within you, and thank the shadow for showing you the way, as a good friend who shows the right way in the darkness.

Shadows can show you the path to liberation, for is this not the purpose of life itself, to be free from the cycles of life — suffering and death?

In the grand journey of life and realization, seek both beings within you — your true self and your shadow self. By embracing both, you will be uplifted and healed. You will become one.

Do not chase away the shadow self; rather, seek it in the deep recesses of your mind. Embrace it, and love it so that this wound within you can heal, and you will set yourself free.

Freedom is what your soul seeks, for freedom is another word for God.

Without the night, there is no day, and in the same way, without the shadow, there is no light.

MASTER RUMI ON

Prayer

Prayer is a science, and in this science, there is mystery and magic. The truth of the universe is embedded in the prayers. A true prayer is one in which the beings in the prayer are invoked.

Prayer is a soothing balm for the soul and a comfort in distress. It was intended to be a bringer of hope and solace during troubled times when humanity was afraid.

Prayer makes you humble and wise, and it creates an opening in the heart to allow the Divine to appear.

Praying is how you surrender to the Creator; you listen with your heart and soul for an answer to your queries of every day.

Prayer is like the water that nourishes all the plants and flowers. It acts as a soothing cream on wintery, parched skin.

Sing the prayer with devotion and humility, and hear the utterances of the soul and Creator. In this, you will find solutions and miracles.

Prayer is like an ocean current that takes your utterances to the bosom of the Creator so that you could be nourished and reborn with the wisdom of the soul and heart.

Prayer is like rosary beads strung together on a single thread. Prayer acts like a bridge between your soul and your higher power.

Prayer is like the beautiful melody of a lute, and when sung in harmony, it lifts you into the heart of the universe.

Prayer is the key to your salvation and freedom, for in prayer, you find faith and courage to move on.

Prayer acts like a string on a kite that lets you fly to greater heights.

Prayer unites and solidifies, and it lets you see the illusion by opening your inner vision.

Prayer sung in the morning and evening has greater power, for these are powerful times when your body is in harmony with the universe and its ever-changing motions. Recite the prayer aloud or in silence, but pray nonetheless.

Prayer spoken in devotion and gratitude is the highest form of prayer, for when you thank the Creator in advance for what you ask, you already have created in the continuum of time and space.

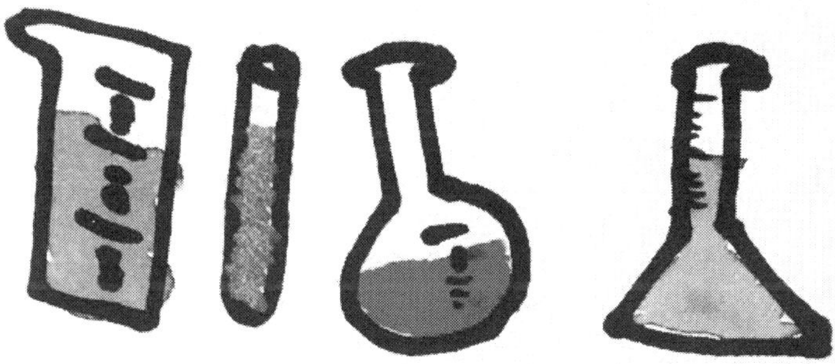

Now it is only a matter of time that you draw it forth into your reality.
Pray for yourself.
Pray for others.
Pray for all humanity.
Pray for Earth and all who are upon it.
In this, you will fulfill a part of your divine dharma.

MASTER RUMI ON

Sunsets

In the evening, I gazed at the sky, and its magnificence dazzled me, for there were brilliant colors in all shades, bright and beautiful for the eyes to behold.

I wondered whether it was the face of God, in his beauty and glory, and I wept with joy as I was filled with a deep sense of peace.

I danced in this dazzling beauty to my heart's desire. This awakened love within me, and my heart sang a song of gratitude and glory, for I was in the process of discovering the secrets of the universe.

I felt humble and serene in this awesome discovery through the beauty of the sunset. I realized that I carry this awesome beauty within me, and I am the Sun within me — with all its colors and beauty. This was always there in the temple of my body.

The sunset is the forebear of the beautiful night sky waiting for its beauty to be displayed. The gentle night, with its indigo beauty, heralds the awakening of many of God's creatures, for their day is just beginning.

Welcome all the displays of God in their beauty, for there is purpose in all. In uniting all, a grand symphony is created by this master musician — God.

Sunset and sunrise open the door to a new way. These times program your body to their beautiful rhythms to enhance your life, making you vital and strong. Your body needs both, and your rhythm is set to these changes.

Colors in the sunset and sunrise remind you of the intricate patterns you were created from, for there are many secrets in your making.

You are a composite of colors, sound, frequency, numbers, patterns, and rhythms all woven into a beautiful tapestry. If you were to see this from above you, it would look like the night sky painted with the most glorious colors.

Embrace these colors, for they can enhance you and nourish you, and they can reset your emotions and well-being in all your bodies — physical, mental, emotional, and spiritual.

MASTER RUMI ON

Faith

Faith is the love and wisdom of God displayed in action.

Faith cannot be seen; it can only be felt and realized, for faith is like the gentle wind that caresses your hair, and in the knowingness, the air that caresses you is always around you.

Faith carries you in your journey of life through tough times and joyful times.

Faith is the harbinger of peace and tranquility, and when you have faith, you have trust. Then you discover hope, and hope brings courage and forbearance, and in that knowingness, a new beginning awaits you.

Faith is like the boat that carries you through the swift currents of a fast moving river. It is also like a boat's sail that helps you glide during the raging times of your life.

Faith brings peace during times of calamity, fear, and anxiety. Faith acts as an anchor to hold on to courage.

You script all the sorrows and joys in your life long before you were born, and faith helps you to discover the acts and the plot.

Faith is a little one's courage to cross the street, and faith is an adult's courage to take the giant leap into the unknown.

Faith is the guiding light that shows the way on a dark night.

Faith is the strength to climb the highest mountain, to seek the unknown, and discover new pastures.

Humans are explorers by nature, and faith has pushed many to discover more of themselves, as well as the many miracles and beauty you see in this world. These were all created by the faith you have in yourselves.

Make faith your good friend and companion, and explore the many mysteries of life and the universe. In this, you will expand and bloom like a gigantic flower whose fragrance will touch all.

Nature and faith are synonymous. Each knows that everything is in perfection.

The universe is in a continuous process of creation and self-discovery. Faith will help you cross over without fear and doubt, knowing full well that there is only light at the end of the tunnel.

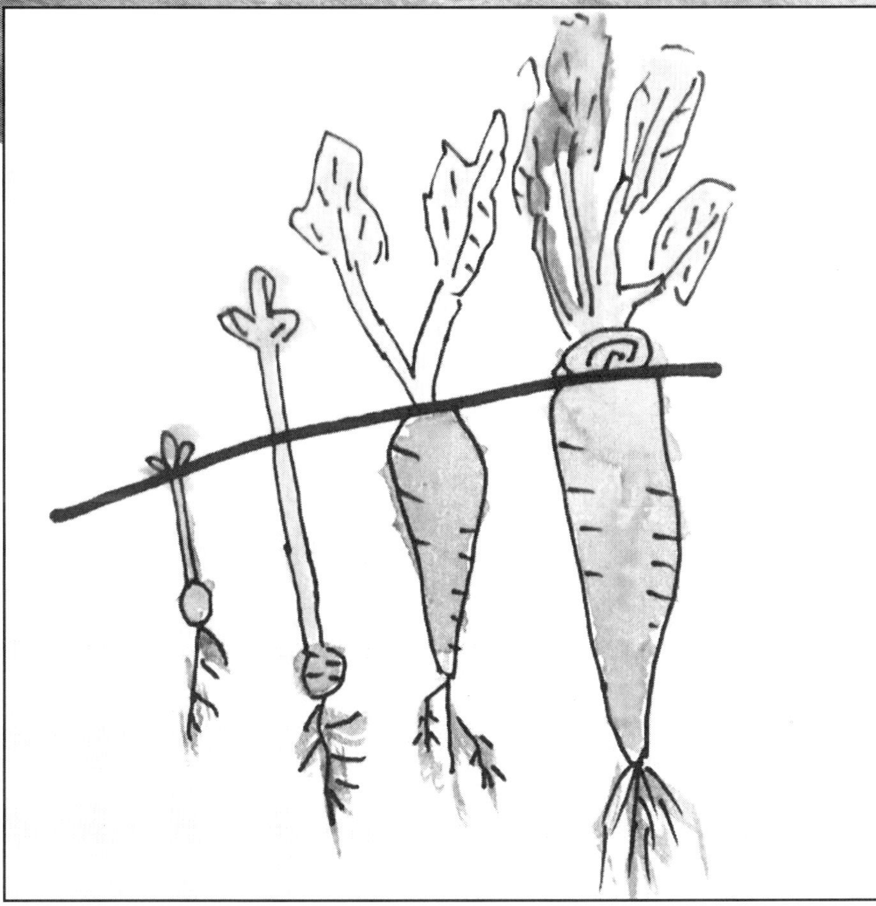

Trust, courage, love, and hope all stem from faith.
Trust lets you roam in your inner strength.
Courage lets you turn your dreams into reality.
Love lets you experience all that you have created.
Hope lets you dream your biggest dreams.
Faith lets you soar above the clouds.

MASTER RUMI ON

Angels

Angels, what are they? Aren't they God's helpers helping humanity? All scriptures speak about them, and they have been here supporting humanity for eons.

Each of you has your personal angels. When you call on them, they are with you in a flash, supporting you and guiding you in more ways than you can imagine.

Angels do not have color or wings, for they are the pure embodiment of love in service to humanity and others. They have been serving Earth and humanity for millennia.

Angels sing a beautiful harmony, and their celestial voices can uplift all who hear them.

They are present when you are born and also when you leave, for they are here to comfort you in your pain and sorrow. Invite them into your home and life, and you will see your life change for the better.

Angels only desire to help and support you in all you do. There are angels for all.

There are angels of seasons and of colors, angels of rainbows and rain, angels of fish and fowl, angels of animals and birds, angels of Earth and the stars, angels of business and commerce, and angels of well-being.

Angels, angels, bestow your love and support on humanity! There is much darkness on Earth now, and the fight between the light and shadow is fierce.

There is fear and anxiety in the human heart. Angels give humanity strength and courage to face the world and to seek the truth within, for they are in the process of making a new world — a world of sharing, equality, compassion, and kindness.

A golden age is being created, and a new road is being constructed. Angels, be with humanity in their sleep and wakefulness, lest they forget their divine duty.

Earth has shifted, and humans need all the support and help they can get in these changing times.

MASTER RUMI ON

The Celestial Soul

Like the blazing light of the bright Sun, my soul shines brilliantly, covering my entire being and all of creation.

This light penetrates the darkest part of my being, bringing with it a sense of grace and well-being.

In temples and places of worship, you see candles and lights burning, and this represents the light of our souls waiting to be awakened. Once awakened, the brilliance of it will erase the illusion and the shadow within us.

You are an eternal soul, and you are the spark of light birthed from the heart of the Creator, bringing with it truth and wisdom.

When you have wisdom, the darkness is banished, and you feel liberated from the heavy burden of karma.

Your celestial soul, the divine director of your life, is ever in your heart, guiding and directing you in the fulfilment of your divine destiny. Your celestial soul guides you gently in the liberation of your life from the eternal cycle of birth and death.

Call forth your celestial soul, and partake of its immense wisdom. Drink from the overflowing cup of love that it offers.

"Celestial soul, celestial soul, I call forth your divine form to guide me so that I can walk in the play I have scripted without bruises and hurts.

"Gently hold my hand, and be my companion in this dark world, lest I forget who I am, for then I would curse the darkness around me, and I would be lost for a long time.

"Celestial soul, celestial soul, gently guide me to be awake so that I can use your guidance for my brothers and sisters. I know that my celestial soul is part of them too.

"Help me walk the path of truth and compassion, and when I am lost, show me the way as the friend that is always on my shoulder, whispering words of encouragement and hope.

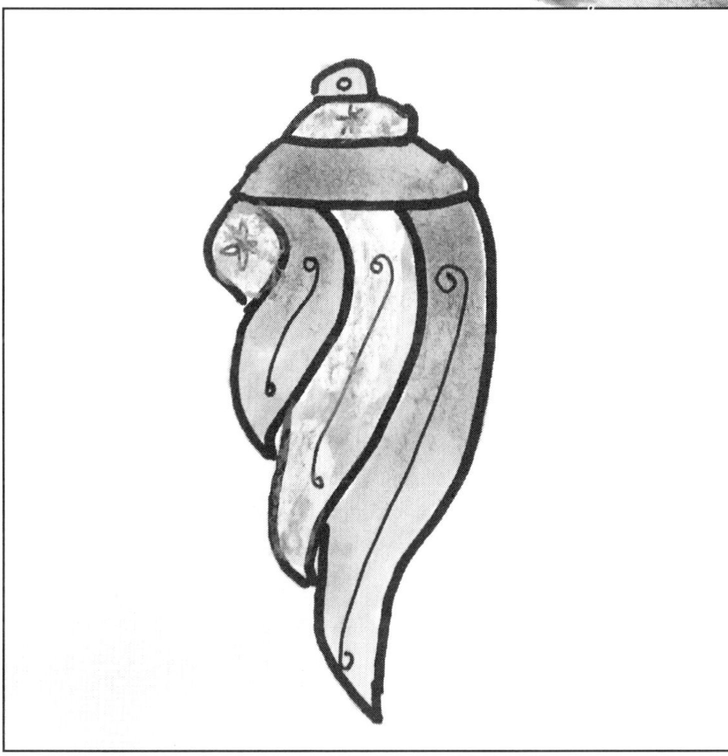

"Celestial soul, celestial soul, let your eyes be my eyes so that I may see only beauty and love in others; so that I may speak lovingly, humbly, and truthfully; and so that I may be a light for others in their darkness.

"Celestial soul, celestial soul, teach me the song of my heart and the holy symphony that I have only heard of, for my heart longs for it, and this ache has been growing and growing.

"I long to be in your loving arms, my beloved celestial soul."

MASTER RUMI ON

The Song of Love

A butterfly flew past me one spring day, and I held its beauty in my heart. I whispered softly, "How beautiful it would be to hold this beautiful butterfly in my arms to cherish its beauty."

Then my heart sang a song of incredible beauty, and I was answered: "It shall be so."

That is how the spring passed — in the glory of life and love — for this beautiful butterfly landed on my heart and asked me, "Is your heart open, dear, to accept me?"

I softly whispered, "Yes," and then I felt a tug at my heart, and I knew love had penetrated me deeply. I felt a stirring within my entire being, and tears flowed from my eyes — the tears of love, joy, and gratitude, for I knew then that I was embraced by a magical and mystical love.

I sang my song of love, and love answered, "How sweet it is to be loved back by you."

My heart cried and said, "The greatest gift in life is to love and be loved in return."

I understood, and I became still. In this stillness, the intensity of this love magnified several hundred times, and I was in ecstasy and bliss. I was in rapture, and this moved me to the stars and the cosmos so that I could dance again in the universe.

CHANNEL

Rae Chandran

Rae Chandran was born in India and has lived in the United States and Japan. He performs personal channeling sessions for his clients, and his articles have been published in the *Sedona Journal of Emergence*. Rae teaches workshops throughout the Far East on the Ancient Egyptian mysteries, DNA activation, and channeling. He creates soul symbols for his clients, and he leads tours of ancient holy places worldwide.

Rae founded the Omran Institute, which promotes DNA awareness and certifies practitioners of Omran 12-Strand DNA Activation. He also performs personal Omran 12-Strand DNA sessions for his clients. Rae lives with his wife and children outside of Tokyo, Japan. For more information, visit his website at www.RaeChandran.com.

ARTIST

Yizhao Zhang

Creative artist and mindfulness Teacher Yizhao Zhang created the artwork for this book. To know more about her and her work, please contact her through LinkedIn.

Light Technology PUBLISHING **Presents**

TO ORDER PRINT BOOKS

Visit LightTechnology.com, Call 928-526-1345 or 1-800-450-0985,
or Check Amazon.com or Your Favorite Bookstore

THROUGH RAE CHANDRAN

$19.95 • Softcover • 384 PP. • ISBN: 978-1-62233-013-3

32 color pages of mudras and images to activate your 12 levels of DNA

DNA of the Spirit, Volume 1

The etheric strands of your DNA are the information library of your soul. They contain the complete history of you, lifetime after lifetime; a record of the attitudes, karma, and emotional predispositions you brought into this lifetime; and a blueprint, or lesson plan, for your self-improvement. Your DNA is also a record of your existence from the moment of your creation as a starbeing to your present incarnation. This information is written in every cell of your body.

CHAPTERS INCLUDE

- Mudras for Activating the Twelve Layers of DNA
- The Awakening of Crystalline Consciousness
- Auspicious Times for Awakening Consciousness
- Angelic Support for DNA Activation
- The History of Human DNA
- Your Internal Compass: Nature's Body Intelligence

All Our Books Are Also Available as eBooks on Amazon, Apple iTunes, Google Play, Barnes & Noble, and Kobo.

Light Technology PUBLISHING Presents

TO ORDER PRINT BOOKS
Visit LightTechnology.com, Call 928-526-1345 or 1-800-450-0985,
or Check Amazon.com or Your Favorite Bookstore

THROUGH RAE CHANDRAN

$16.95 • Softcover • 192 PP. • 978-1-62233-027-0

DNA of the Spirit, Volume 2

This companion book to *DNA of the Spirit, Volume 1* originated with the intention and desire to bring forth understanding to support humanity. Go through this volume while holding a sacredness inside of you, asking that the material be imprinted in your sacredness so that it may become an experience that you will be able to live.

Some of the material in this book is coded, and sincere students will find they can open these codes. Understanding can be received through your own filter and in your own way. This way, you will find the Divine within.

CHAPTERS INCLUDE

- Auric Imprinting Technique for Healing
- The Number of God
- Reveal Your Life Contracts
- Re-create Your Life with Your Akashic Records
- Humans Are Creators in Training
- Use Shape-Shifting for Regeneration
- How to Activate the Codes Within You
- From Darkness unto Light: the Aquarian Age
- Discover Your Energy Connections to Beings of Light
- Understand the Sacred Geometry of the Human Body
- Determine What Drives Your Soul

All Our Books Are Also Available as eBooks on Amazon, Apple iTunes, Google Play, Barnes & Noble, and Kobo.

Light Technology PUBLISHING **Presents**

TO ORDER PRINT BOOKS

Visit LightTechnology.com, Call 928-526-1345 or 1-800-450-0985, or Check Amazon.com or Your Favorite Bookstore

THROUGH RAE CHANDRAN

$16.95 • Softcover • 208 PP. • 978-1-62233-034-8

CHAPTERS INCLUDE

- The Benefits of Working with Angels
- Prepare for a New Consciousness
- Design Your Unique Path
- Access Support from Celestial Bodies
- Invoke Vibrational Support and Activation
- Practice Universal Communication
- Develop Environmental Connections
- You Are the New Masters

Partner with Angels and Benefit Every Area of Your Life

Angels are the Creator's workforce, and in this book, individual angels describe their responsibilities and explain how they can help you with all aspects of your life — practical and spiritual. All you need to do is ask.

Many of these angels have never spoken to human beings before or revealed their names or what they do. Here are some examples of what you will find inside:

- **La Banaha**, the essence of the Moon, explains feminine empowerment and organ rejuvenation.
- **Angel Anauel** describes fair commerce.
- **Angel Tahariel** helps you purify and shift your vibration.
- **Angel Mansu** gives advice about how to eliminate the trauma from birthing procedures.
- **Angel Agon** inspires writers and filmmakers and relates how you can call on him for inspiration.
- **Angel Tadzekiel** helps you access your own wisdom and put it into perspective.
- **Archangel Maroni** downloads your individual pathway to ascension.

The purpose of this material is to bring the awareness of angels in a much more practical, easy-to-understand way. Call on the angels to show you the potential you have in your life to create a new reality.

Light Technology PUBLISHING Presents

TO ORDER PRINT BOOKS

Visit LightTechnology.com, Call 928-526-1345 or 1-800-450-0985,
or Check Amazon.com or Your Favorite Bookstore

THROUGH RAE CHANDRAN

DANCE OF THE HANDS

Dance of the Hands is for everyone, not just people who are spiritually advanced. It is for any layperson, regardless of religion. This material is for those who have an interest in bettering themselves or improving their well-being — practitioners, teachers, masters, the spiritually advanced, neophytes, and children.

The purpose of these mudras is to balance the body, mind, and soul. Like any spiritual practice, doing mudras brings balance to every area of your life. The benefits are simple as well: These mudras bring joy and peace to your life. When you are joyful and peaceful, you are more likely to access the higher aspects of your consciousness.

Practicing these mudras can bring you a sense of calmness, well-being, and heightened awareness. Each person will have individual results. Over time, you will notice a sense of balance and empowerment coming into your life. Relationships can be healed and reconciled. You will become more tolerant, more accepting, and less judgmental.

$16.95 • Softcover • 160 PP. • 978-1-62233-038-6
Lay flat book with wire-o binding

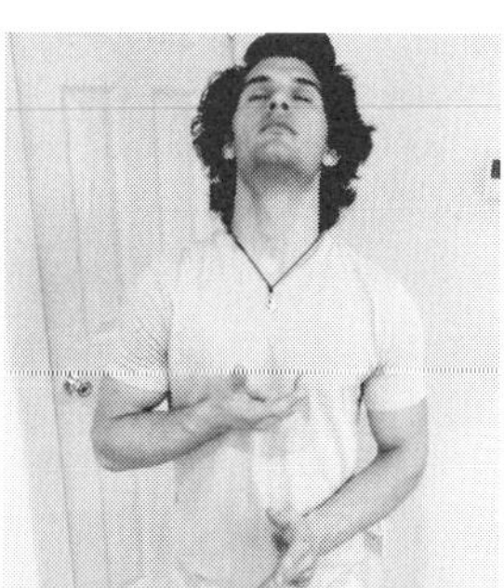

I Am the Presence

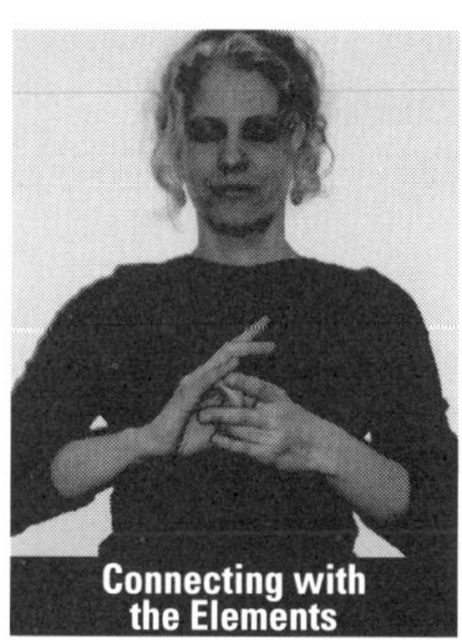

Connecting with the Elements

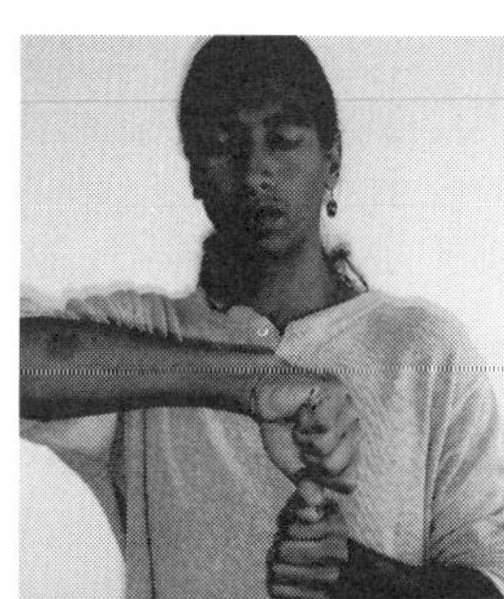

Courage

All Our Books Are Also Available as eBooks on Amazon, Apple iTunes, Google Play, Barnes & Noble, and Kobo.

THROUGH RAE CHANDRAN

$16.95 • Softcover • 6 x 9 • 176 PP. • 978-1-62233-048-5

Includes Mudras, Breathing Exercises, and Intonations!

CHAPTERS INCLUDE

- Enhance Your Senses and Vitality
- Boost Your Mental Facilities
- Expand Your Consciousness
- Use Numbers to Improve Your Life
- Find Your Blueprint and Life Plan
- Clear Karmic Energy
- Spiritual Cosmology

Angels and Ascension

Integrate Celestial Energy for a Benevolent Life

Much support is available for humanity. Angelic support has always been available, but people did not know about it because they were looking for a tangible support system — something they could see, feel, or touch. In the new consciousness, you must learn to believe in the unseen. Know support is available if you focus.

The angels completely support every human soul on the planet as well as all animals, plants, and trees, but you must ask for this support system to be activated. We bring the understanding of angels so that you can work with them to find joy, peace, and freedom in your heart. We encourage you to speak with all your friends and family about the benefits of working with angels. Work with angels every day, and you will see the difference.

Light Technology PUBLISHING **Presents**

TO ORDER PRINT BOOKS

Visit LightTechnology.com, Call 928-526-1345 or 1-800-450-0985,
or Check Amazon.com or Your Favorite Bookstore

BOOKS THROUGH ROBERT SHAPIRO

Practical Spirituality Series

Benevolent Magic & Living Prayer

This first book in the Feminine Science series provides an easy-to-read, introduction to benevolent magic and living prayer.

$9.95 • 3.75 x 5 • Softcover • 96 PP.
978-1-891824-49-4

THE MINI BOOK OF transformation

Topics Include:

Heart Love/Heart Heat • Clearing
Disentanglement • Deep Disentanglement
Disentanglement Clearings • and much more!

— Learn how to ask for clearing of old traumas and discomforts.
— Learn how to clear yourself so you can create a nourishing, benevolent life for yourself and others.

$9.95 • 3.75 x 5 • Softcover
978-1-62233-029-4

All Our Books Are Also Available as eBooks on Amazon, Apple iTunes, Google Play, and Barnes & Noble.

Light Technology PUBLISHING Presents

TO ORDER PRINT BOOKS
Visit LightTechnology.com, Call 928-526-1345 or 1-800-450-0985,
or Check Amazon.com or Your Favorite Bookstore

THROUGH TINA LOUISE SPALDING

MAKING LOVE TO GOD

The Path to Divine Sex

"We have never seen more hurt and lonely people anywhere than on this planet at the moment. You are all in such a state that we have come from far and wide, from different times and places, to teach you how to relieve the deep suffering you are in. And indeed, it is in the bedroom, in your relationships to yourself, your lover, and God, that these hurts began.

"We are here to teach the way to divine bliss, and we know you are scared — scared to lie naked caressing your lover with rapt attention and honor. We know you are scared to kiss and connect, to feel such deep connection and pleasure that the ego starts to get very nervous, sensing the threat to the well-guarded and limited access to your heart that it deems to be safe.

"If we can turn the tide of thought in enough people, there will be a revolution of love on the planet, the likes of which you have never seen. Relationships will stabilize, marriages will last, and the passion and joy you so wish to experience will become manifest wherever you look."

— Ananda

$19.95 Softcover, 416 PP.
ISBN 978-1-62233-009-6

Topics Include

- How We Came to Misunderstand Sexual Energy
- Using Divine Sex Energy
- Specific Steps and Sensations
- Blocks to Transformation
- A Transformed View of Sex and Sexual Energy
- Following the Path to Transformation
- Reaping the Harvest

All Our Books Are Also Available as eBooks on Amazon, Apple iTunes, Google Play, Barnes & Noble, and Kobo.

Light Technology PUBLISHING Presents

TO ORDER PRINT BOOKS
Visit LightTechnology.com, Call 928-526-1345 or 1-800-450-0985,
or Check Amazon.com or Your Favorite Bookstore

THROUGH TINA LOUISE SPALDING

LOVE AND A MAP TO THE UNALTERED SOUL

"True love is never-ending. It does not refuse or inflict punishment, it does not withdraw or have temper tantrums, and it does not punish. Love always is, and it always emits the same high frequency of absolute, unconditional caring and offering, of growing and creation."

— Ananda

$16.95 Softcover, 240 PP.
ISBN 978-1-62233-047-8

We think we know what love is, but in *Love and a Map to the Unaltered Soul*, we are challenged to broaden our definition and free ourselves from constraints we never realized we had. In these pages, you will learn that love is a process of climbing your ladder of consciousness. Through Tina Louise Spalding, the beings Ananda, Jesus, and Mary Magdalene give practical instruction and examples on how to find and keep love at the center of your life.

CHAPTERS INCLUDE

- The Unaltered Soul Seeks Experience
- Move beyond the Physical
- You Are Part of a Greater Oneness
- You Can Raise Your Frequency
- Seek Love Within
- You Create Your Experiences
- How to Find Love
- Align with Love to Find Happiness
- Question Your Beliefs
- Implement Healthy Routines
- The Choice Is Yours
- Forgiveness Demonstrates Love

All Our Books Are Also Available as eBooks on Amazon, Apple iTunes, Google Play, Barnes & Noble, and Kobo.

Light Technology PUBLISHING Presents

TO ORDER PRINT BOOKS

Visit LightTechnology.com, Call 928-526-1345 or 1-800-450-0985, or Check Amazon.com or Your Favorite Bookstore

BY TOM T. MOORE

THE GENTLE WAY

A SELF-HELP GUIDE FOR THOSE WHO BELIEVE IN ANGELS

"This book is for people of all faiths and beliefs with the only requirement being a basic belief in angels. It will put you back in touch with your guardian angel or strengthen and expand the connection that you may already have. How can I promise these benefits? Because I have been using these concepts for over ten years and I can report these successes from direct knowledge and experience. But this is a self-help guide, so that means it requires your active participation." —Tom T. Moore

$14.95 • 160 pp., Softcover • ISBN 978-1-891824-60-9

THE GENTLE WAY II

BENEVOLENT OUTCOMES: THE STORY CONTINUES

You'll be amazed at how easy it is to be in touch with guardian angels and how much assistance you can receive simply by asking. This inspirational self-help book, written for all faiths and beliefs, explains how there is a more benevolent world that we can access and how we can achieve this.

This unique and incredibly simple technique assists you in manifesting your goals easily and effortlessly for the first time. It works quickly, sometimes with immediate results, and no affirmations, written intentions, or changes in behavior are needed. You don't even have to believe in it for it to work!

$16.95 • 320 pp., Softcover • ISBN 978-1-891824-80-7

THE GENTLE WAY III

MASTER YOUR LIFE

"Almost three years have passed since *The Gentle Way II* was published. Yet as many success stories as that book contained, I have continued to receive truly unique stories from people all over the world requesting most benevolent outcomes and asking for benevolent prayers for their families, friends, other people, and other beings. It just proves that there are no limits to this modality, which is becoming a gentle movement as people discover how much better their lives are with these simple yet powerful requests." — Tom T. Moore

$16.95 • 352 pp., Softcover • ISBN 978-1-62233-005-8

All Our Books Are Also Available as eBooks on Amazon, Apple iTunes, Google Play, Barnes & Noble, and Kobo.

Light Technology PUBLISHING Presents

TO ORDER PRINT BOOKS

Visit LightTechnology.com, Call 928-526-1345 or 1-800-450-0985,
or Check Amazon.com or Your Favorite Bookstore

THROUGH KRYON

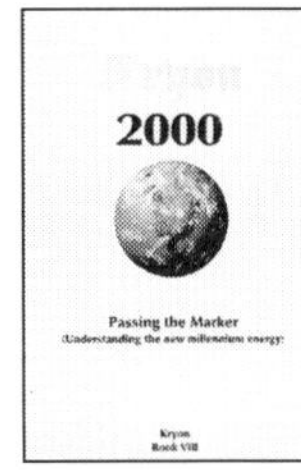

Kryon (Book 1):
The End Times
$12.00 • Softcover
176 PP.
978-0-9636304-2-1

Kryon (Book 2):
Don't Think Like a Human!
$12.00 • Softcover
288 PP.
978-0-9636304-0-7

Kryon (Book 5):
The Journey Home
$13.95 • Softcover
258 PP.
978-1-56170-552-8

Kryon (Book 6):
Partnering with God
$14.00 • Softcover
400 PP.
978-1-888053-10-4

Kryon (Book 8):
Passing the Marker
$14.00 • Softcover
424 PP.
978-1-888053-11-1

Kryon (Book 10):
A New Dispensation
$14.98 • Softcover
408 PP.
978-1-888053-14-2

Kryon (Book 11):
Lifting the Veil
$14.98 • Softcover
384 PP.
978-1-888053-19-7

Kryon (Book 12):
The Twelve Layers of DNA
$16.98 • Softcover
336 PP.
978-1-933465-05-0

Kryon (Book 13):
The Recalibration of Humanity
$16.98 • Softcover
264 PP.
978-1-8888053-22-4

Kryon (Book 14):
The New Human
$16.95 • Softcover
248 PP.
978-1-8888053-20-3

An Indigo Celebration
$13.95 • Softcover
252 PP.
978-1-56170-859-8

The Indigo Children
$13.95 • Softcover
272 PP.
978-1-56170-608-2

The Indigo Children Ten Years Later
$15.95 • Softcover
312 PP.
978-1-4019-2317-4

All Our Books Are Also Available as eBooks on Amazon, Apple iTunes, Google Play, Barnes & Noble, and Kobo.

Light Technology PUBLISHING **Presents**

TO ORDER PRINT BOOKS

Visit LightTechnology.com, Call 928-526-1345 or 1-800-450-0985, or Check Amazon.com or Your Favorite Bookstore

THROUGH ROBERT SHAPIRO

Are You a Walk-In?

Book 19

From the walk-in's perspective, the benefit of this new form of birth is coming into an adult body and being able to bring one's gifts to humanity without having to take the time to go through the usual birth process. The other side of this is that the walk-in has to resolve the physical, emotional, and spiritual issues that the walk-out left behind in order to completely express its own personality.

"This book is intended to be practical advice for day-to-day living for people who know they are walk-ins, for people who believe they might be walk-ins, or for the family and friends and business associates of people who are believed to be walk-ins. In short, this book is intended to serve the community to understand the walk-in phenomenon and for those who are experiencing it personally to be able to apply it in such a way as they are able to live easier, more comfortable, more useful, and more fulfilling lives."

— Reveals the Mysteries

$19.95 • Softcover • 304 PP.

ISBN 978-1-891824-40-1

Chapters Include

- How the Body Prepares for a New Soul
- The Physical Effects of the Walk-In Experience
- Communication between the Exiting Soul and the Walk-In
- Walk-In or Soul Braid
- Walking in, a Benevolent Birth Process
- How the Walk-In Adjusts
- Your Walk-In Experience Is Supported by Your Physical Body
- How to Live as a Walk-In

All Our Books Are Also Available as eBooks on Amazon, Apple iTunes, Google Play, Barnes & Noble, and Kobo.

Light Technology PUBLISHING Presents

TO ORDER PRINT BOOKS
Visit LightTechnology.com, Call 928-526-1345 or 1-800-450-0985,
or Check Amazon.com or Your Favorite Bookstore

THROUGH ROBERT SHAPIRO

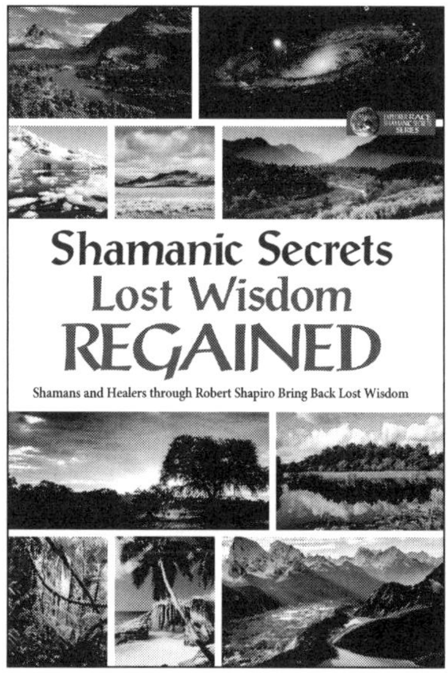

$16.95 • Softcover
6 x 9 • 352 PP.
978-1-62233-049-2

Shamanic Secrets Lost Wisdom Regained

Due to wars, natural disasters, a shaman not being able to train a successor, and many other reasons, Isis (through Robert) says that 95 percent of the accumulated shamanic wisdom has been lost. Now it is important to regain this wisdom as young people who are able to learn and use these processes are being born now.

Beings who lived as shamans and healers on Earth at various times now speak through Robert Shapiro and bring these lost teachings and techniques to a humanity waking up and discovering it has the talents and abilities to use this wisdom for the benefit of all.

Chapters Include

- Bring Life Back to Your Drinking Water
- Look to Plants and Animals for Health and Wellness Clues
- Hold in Your Heart the Values of All Life
- Share Your Healing Wisdom with Others
- Work as a Group for the Benefit of All
- Collect Healing Energy from the Stars
- Accept and Maintain Your Physical Body

All Our Books Are Also Available as eBooks on Amazon, Apple iTunes, Google Play, Barnes & Noble, and Kobo.

Light Technology PUBLISHING **Presents**

TO ORDER PRINT BOOKS

Visit LightTechnology.com, Call 928-526-1345 or 1-800-450-0985,
or Check Amazon.com or Your Favorite Bookstore

THROUGH DRUNVALO MELCHIZEDEK

THE ANCIENT SECRET OF THE FLOWER OF LIFE, VOLUME 1

Once, all life in the universe knew the Flower of Life as the creation pattern, the geometrical design leading us into and out of physical existence. Then from a very high state of consciousness, we fell into darkness, the secret hidden for thousands of years, encoded in the cells of all life.

Now we are rising from the darkness, and a new dawn is streaming through the windows of perception. This book is one of those windows. Drunvalo Melchizedek presents in text and graphics the Flower of Life workshop, illuminating the mysteries of how we came to be.

Sacred geometry is the form beneath our being and points to a divine order in our reality. We can follow that order from the invisible atom to the infinite stars, finding ourselves at each step. The information here is one path, but between the lines and drawings lie the feminine gems of intuitive understanding.

You may see them sparkle around some of these provocative ideas:

- remembering our ancient past
- the secret of the Flower unfolds
- the darker side of our present/past
- the geometries of the human body
- the significance of shape and structure

$25.00 Softcover, 240 pp.
ISBN 978-1-891824-17-3

Drunvalo Melchizedek's life experience reads like an encyclopedia of breakthroughs in human endeavor. He studied physics and art at the University of California, Berkeley, but he feels that his most important education came after college. In the past twenty-five years, he has studied with over seventy teachers from all belief systems and religious understandings. For some time now, he has been bringing his vision to the world through the Flower of Life program and the Mer-Ka-Ba meditation. This teaching encompasses every area of human understanding, explores the development of humankind from ancient civilizations to the present time, and offers clarity regarding the world's state of consciousness and what is needed for a smooth and easy transition into the twenty-first century.

All Our Books Are Also Available as eBooks on Amazon, Apple iTunes, Google Play, Barnes & Noble, and Kobo.

Light Technology PUBLISHING Presents

TO ORDER PRINT BOOKS

Visit LightTechnology.com, Call 928-526-1345 or 1-800-450-0985,
or Check Amazon.com or Your Favorite Bookstore

THROUGH DRUNVALO MELCHIZEDEK

THE ANCIENT SECRET OF THE FLOWER OF LIFE, VOLUME 2

The sacred Flower of Life pattern, the primary geometric generator of all physical form, is explored in even more depth in this volume, the second half of the famed Flower of Life workshop. The proportions of the human body; the nuances of human consciousness; the sizes and distances of the stars, planets, and moons; and even the creations of humankind are all shown to reflect their origins in this beautiful and divine image. Through an intricate and detailed geometrical mapping, Drunvalo Melchizedek shows how the seemingly simple design of the Flower of Life contains the genesis of our entire third-dimensional existence.

From the pyramids and mysteries of Egypt to the new race of Indigo children, Drunvalo presents the sacred geometries of the reality and the subtle energies that shape our world. We are led through a divinely inspired labyrinth of science and stories, logic and coincidence, on a path of remembering where we come from and the wonder and magic of who we are.

Finally, for the first time in print, Drunvalo shares the instructions for the Mer-Ka-Ba meditation, step-by-step techniques for the re-creation of the energy field of the evolved human, which is the key to ascension and the next dimensional world. If done from love, this ancient process of breathing prana opens up for us a world of tantalizing possibility in this dimension, from protective powers to the healing of oneself, others, and even the planet.

Topics Include

- The Unfolding of the Third Informational System
- Whispers from Our Ancient Heritage
- Unveiling the Mer-Ka-Ba Meditation
- Using Your Mer-Ka-Ba
- Connecting to the Levels of Self
- Two Cosmic Experiments
- What We May Expect in the Forthcoming Dimensional Shift

$25.00 Softcover, 272 pp.
ISBN 978-1-891824-21-0

All Our Books Are Also Available as eBooks on Amazon, Apple iTunes, Google Play, Barnes & Noble, and Kobo.

Light Technology PUBLISHING Presents

TO ORDER PRINT BOOKS

Visit LightTechnology.com, Call 928-526-1345 or 1-800-450-0985, or Check Amazon.com or Your Favorite Bookstore

BOOKS FOR CHILDREN FROM LEIA STINNETT

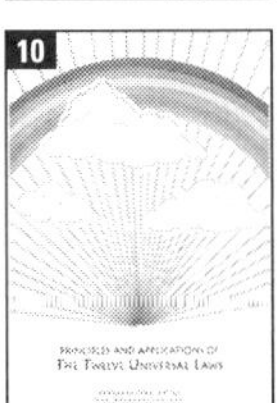

1. **All My Angel Friends (Coloring Book)**
   $10.95 • Softcover • 64 PP.
   978-0-929385-80-8

2. **The Angel Told Me to Tell You Good-Bye**
   $6.95 • Softcover • 64 PP.
   978-0-929385-84-6

3. **Animal Tales: Spiritual Lessons from Our Animal Friends**
   $7.95 • Softcover • 96 PP.
   978-0-929385-96-9

4. **The Bridge between Two Worlds**
   $6.95 • Softcover • 64 PP.
   978-0-929385-85-3

5. **A Circle of Angels (Workbook)**
   $18.95 • Softcover • 112 PP.
   978-0-929385-87-7

6. **Color Me One**
   $6.95 • Softcover • 64 PP.
   978-0-929385-82-2

7. **Just Lighten Up! (Coloring Book)**
   $9.95 • Softcover • 48 PP.
   978-0-929385-64-8

8. **The Little Angel Who Could Not Fly**
   $9.95 • Softcover • 64 PP.
   978-1-62233-025-6

9. **One Red Rose**
   $6.95 • Softcover • 64 PP.
   978-0-929385-83-9

10. **Principles and Applications of the Twelve Universal Laws**
    $18.95 • Softcover • 128 PP.
    978-0-929385-81-5

11. **When the Earth Was New**
    $6.95 • Softcover • 64 PP.
    978-0-929385-91-4

12. **Where Is God?**
    $6.95 • Softcover • 64 PP.
    978-0-929385-90-7

13. **Who's Afraid of the Dark?**
    $6.95 • Softcover • 64 PP.
    978-0-929385-89-1

14. **Exploring the Chakras**
    $6.95 • Softcover • 64 PP.
    978-0-929385-86-0

15. **Crystals R for Kids**
    $6.95 • Softcover • 64 PP.
    978-0-929385-92-1

16. **Happy Feet**
    $6.95 • Softcover • 64 PP.
    978-0-929385-88-4

All Our Books Are Also Available as eBooks on Amazon, Apple iTunes, Google Play, Barnes & Noble, and Kobo.

Light Technology PUBLISHING Presents

SEDONA JOURNAL OF Emergence

ORDER NOW

to receive SPECTACULAR SAVINGS on your *Sedona Journal* subscription!

PRINT SUBSCRIPTIONS

Mailed U.S. Subscriptions

1ST CLASS	2ND CLASS
❒ 2 yrs $129	❒ 2 yrs $79
❒ 1 yr $65	❒ 1 yr $43

Canada

❒ 2 yrs .... $159 ❒ 1 yr $83

All prices are in U.S. currency.

All Other Countries

❒ 2 yrs .... $299 ❒ 1 yr $154

All prices are in U.S. currency.

NOTE: The U.S. Postal Service has changed postal rates, eliminating Canadian and global 2nd class surface and increasing all airmail rates.

Name: ____________________

Address: ____________________

City: ____________ State: ______ Zip: ______

Phone: ____________ Email: ____________

Gift Recipient Name: ____________________

Address: ____________________

City: ____________ State: ______ Zip: ______

Personalized Gift Card from: ____________________

METHOD OF PAYMENT (CHECK ONE):

❒ CHECK ❒ M.O.

❒ VISA ❒ MASTERCARD ❒ DISCOVER ❒ AMEX

CARD NO. ____________________

EXPIRATION DATE ____________________

SIGNATURE ____________________

Subscription includes the annual double-size PREDICTIONS ISSUE at no extra charge.

ELECTRONIC SUBSCRIPTIONS

with Bonus Content

Get the entire journal plus additional content online by subscription — and get it 2 weeks before it hits newsstands!

❒ 2 yrs .... $55 ❒ 1 yr $29

All electronic and combo subscriptions *MUST* be purchased online at *www.SedonaJournal.com* to obtain username and password

Get the Best of Both Worlds!

Special Combo Offers!

U.S.A.

Get BOTH Printed AND Electronic Subscriptions

1ST CLASS	2ND CLASS
❒ 2 yrs $159	❒ 2 yrs $109
❒ 1 yr $81	❒ 1 yr $59

Canada

Get an Airmail Printed Subscription Along with an Electronic Subscription for Only

❒ 2 yrs ...... $189 ❒ 1 yr $99

NOTE: The U.S. Postal Service has changed postal rates, eliminating Canadian and global 2nd class surface and increasing all airmail rates.

All Countries

Get an Airmail Printed Subscription Along with an Electronic Subscription for Only

❒ 2 yrs ...... $329 ❒ 1 yr $170

Order online: www.SedonaJournal.com or call 928-526-1345 or 1-800-450-0985

Light Technology PUBLISHING Presents

EASY ORDER 24 HOURS A DAY

Order ONLINE!
www.lighttechnology.com
Email:
customersrv@
lighttechnology.net

Order by Mail
Send To:
Light Technology Publishing
PO Box 3540
Flagstaff, AZ 86003

Order by Phone
800-450-0985
928-526-1345

Order by Fax
928-714-1132

Available from your favorite bookstore or

LIGHT Technology PUBLISHING

PayPal

www.LightTechnology.com
We Offer the Best Channeled and Inspired Books of Wisdom.
Use Our Secure Checkout.
In-Depth Information on Books, Including Excerpts and Contents.
Use the Links to Our Other Great Sites. See Below.

www.SedonaJournal.com
Read Excerpts of Monthly Channeling and Predictions in Advance.
Use Our Email Links to Contact Us or Send a Submission.
Electronic Subscriptions Available — with or without Print Copies.

www.BenevolentMagic.com
Learn the techniques of benevolence toward self and benevolence toward others to create global peace. Download all the techniques of benevolent magic and living prayer for FREE!

www.ExplorerRace.com
All of humanity constitutes the Explorer Race, volunteers for a grand and glorious experiment. Discover your purpose, your history, and your future. Download the first chapter of each book for FREE!

www.ShamanicSecrets.com
What we call shamanism is the natural way of life for beings on other planets. Learn to be aware of your natural self and your natural talents and abilities. Download the first chapter of each book for FREE!